Circle of Friends

Shared
Friendship

Inspiration for a Woman's Soul

BARBOUR
PUBLISHING

Circle of Friends is a ministry of women helping women. Born out of a small accountability group that led to a women's Bible study, Circle of Friends Ministries is now a nonprofit organization dedicated to encouraging women to find and follow Christ. Our desire is to encourage one another to love God more deeply and to follow Him with a heart of passion that reaches out and draws others along with us on our journey.

"Circle of Friends are women of biblical depth and compassion for others. They have a knack for bringing humor, hope, and practical application to everyday situations."

—Carol Kent, speaker and author
When I Lay My Isaac Down and *A New Kind of Normal*

"Circle of Friends has its finger on the pulse of the heart-needs of women today. Through word and song they link arms with women around the globe to bring the hope and healing of Jesus Christ."

—Sharon Jaynes, speaker and author
Becoming a Woman Who Listens to God and
Extraordinary Moments with God

Scripture quotations marked NASB are taken from the New American Standard Bible, © 1960, 1962, 1963, 1968, 1971, 1972, 1973, 1975, 1977, 1995 by The Lockman Foundation. Used by permission.

Scripture quotations marked NIV are taken from the HOLY BIBLE, NEW INTERNATIONAL VERSION®. NIV®. Copyright © 1973, 1978, 1984, 2010 by Biblica™. Used by permission. All rights reserved worldwide.

Scripture quotations marked NLT are taken from the *Holy Bible*, New Living Translation, copyright © 1996, 2004. Used by permission of Tyndale House Publishers, Inc. Wheaton, Illinois 60189, U.S.A. All rights reserved.

Scripture quotations marked KJV are taken from the King James Version of the Bible.

Scripture quotations marked AMP are taken from the Amplified® Bible, © 1954, 1958, 1962, 1964, 1965, 1987 by The Lockman Foundation. Used by permission.

Scripture quotations marked NKJV are taken from the New King James Version®. Copyright © 1982 by Thomas Nelson, Inc. Used by permission. All rights reserved.

Scripture quotations marked CEV are from the Contemporary English Version, Copyright © 1991, 1992, 1995 by American Bible Society. Used by permission.

Scripture quotations marked ESV are from The Holy Bible, English Standard Version®, copyright © 2001 by Crossway Bibles, a publishing ministry of Good News Publishers. Used by permission. All rights reserved.

Scripture quotations marked MSG are from *THE MESSAGE*. Copyright © by Eugene H. Peterson 1993, 1994, 1995, 1996, 2000, 2001, 2002. Used by permission of NavPress Publishing Group.

Scripture quotations marked NCV are taken from the New Century Version of the Bible, copyright © 2005 by Thomas Nelson, Inc. Used by permission.

Published by Barbour Publishing, Inc., P.O. Box 719, Uhrichsville, Ohio 44683, www.barbourbooks.com

Our mission is to publish and distribute inspirational products offering exceptional value and biblical encouragement to the masses.

Introduction

Who can understand the heart of a woman—with all its joys and triumphs, challenges and heartaches—better than another woman? We are told in the book of Titus that mature women of the faith are able to be "teachers of good things" and in Hebrews that we are to "exhort [encourage] one another daily."

Shared Friendship is a devotional written by women who have a passion and love for Jesus. Their stories, insights, biblical applications, and refreshing honesty in everyday trials in their lives will encourage your faith and strengthen your relationships. So grab a cup of coffee or tea, pull up a chair, and share life, share hope, with your "Circle of Friends." You'll laugh, you'll cry, you'll find that you have truly found a place to belong.

What Is a True Friend?

There are "friends" who destroy each other,
but a real friend sticks closer than a brother.

PROVERBS 18:24 NLT

In today's world we use the term *friend* loosely. Unable to describe a hypothetical, indefinable somebody, we often say, "I have a friend who. . ." The person usually is a distant acquaintance, but because we are unable to determine what to call them, we clump them into the multifaceted category of friend.

An ancient proverb, however, captures the essence and beauty of true friendship. It says, "Ah, the beauty of being at peace with another, neither having to weigh thoughts or measure words, but spilling them out just as they are, chaff and grain together, certain that a faithful hand will keep what is worth keeping and, with a breath of kindness, blow the rest away."

Friends find the good in us and dismiss the rest. We can be ourselves in their presence and not worry about misunderstandings or saying the wrong thing.

Jesus is that kind of friend. He sticks close by us at our most undesirable, least lovable moments. We can tell Him anything and He understands. In fact, He knows everything about us and loves us anyway. Like a true friend, Jesus enhances our good qualities and, with a breath of kindness, blows the rest away.

Tina Krause
Whispers of Wisdom for Busy Women

Intercessors

My intercessor is my friend.
JOB 16:20 NIV

It is wonderful to be called to be intercessors. Anyone can do it! . . . Intercession is important work. Do you know that Isaiah 59:16 says that God was amazed that there was no intercessor? I remember that my sister Betsie and I were once in a Dutch concentration camp in Vught. We were there because we had rescued Jews. One day we thought that we were being called to be released, but, instead, we found ourselves standing in the middle of the concentration camp in front of a bunker that was being used as the jail. Standing to our right and left were prisoners. As we stood there, we realized that we might all be killed.

Suddenly, we noticed that there were no longer any guards. One of the prisoners shouted out, "Is there anyone here who can pray?" Betsie answered, "Yes, I can pray and I will." And she prayed! She prayed for herself, she prayed for the men next to her, she prayed for me, and she thanked the Lord that, even if we were killed, the best was yet to come for those who belonged to the Lord Jesus. She asked the Lord to take our hand if we were about to pass through the valley of the shadow of death. I can't remember what else she prayed, but it was a wonderful prayer. How marvelous it is to intercede.

CORRIE TEN BOOM
REFLECTIONS OF GOD'S GLORY

Friends in Glory

For if we believe that Jesus died and
rose again, even so them also which sleep
in Jesus will God bring with him.

1 Thessalonians 4:14 kjv

Dr. Lowry's health began to fail and we watched him with growing anxiety. I shall always recall our last meeting at his home in Plainfield, New Jersey, with tender emotions. We talked together of many of the events of thirty years, and finally he said, "Fanny, I am going to join those who have gone before, for my work is now done." I could not speak with him concerning the parting without betraying my grief, so I simply took his hand in mine and said quietly, "I thank you, Dr. Lowry, for all that you have done for me; good night, until we meet in the morning." Then I silently went down the stairs, with the impression on my mind that the good man would soon be at rest from his labors, and so indeed it proved.

A little while to weep for those we cherish,
As one by one they near the river's brink;
A little while to catch their sweet assurance,
That we in heaven shall find each missing link;
A little while and then the glorious dawning
Of that fair morn beyond the swelling tide,
When we shall wake and in our Saviour's likeness,
Perfect and pure, we shall be satisfied.

FANNY CROSBY
MEMORIES OF EIGHTY YEARS

What Friends Are For

Two are better than one, because they have a good return
for their labor: If either of them falls down,
one can help the other up.

ECCLESIASTES 4:9–10 NIV

Did you ever notice that there are certain tasks that are
simply hard to get motivated to do? And have you also
noticed that if a friend is part of the equation, it makes
it much easier? Physical exercise, as well as wallpapering
and painting, are tasks that challenge me. Frankly, so was
reading through the Bible back when I realized it was
something I needed to do on a regular basis. But today I
cannot imagine a day without God's Word!

I don't know if I would have persevered without my
accountability group encouraging and motivating me to
read God's Word every day. It was a spiritual exercise that I
tried to do regularly but other things caught my attention,

and typically the loudest "voice" always caught me first. God seldom chooses to yell at us—He just patiently waits, and allows people in our lives who will encourage and motivate us along the way. Perhaps that is why He says in His Word that "two are better than one." He knew that relationships and the accountability they offer are just what we need!

BETH BEECHY
CIRCLE OF FRIENDS

A Godly Guest List

"But when you give a banquet, invite the poor,
the crippled, the lame, the blind, and you will be blessed.
Although they cannot repay you, you will be repaid
at the resurrection of the righteous."

LUKE 14:13–14 NIV

You may not host banquets, but what about barbeques? Dinner parties? Pizza and movie nights? Now we're talking.

It is tempting to carefully select a few people to invite to a dinner party. You know the routine—a close girl friend, a guy she thinks is attractive, a guy you are interested in, and then a couple of "fillers" just so that the plot is not obvious.

The Bible admonishes us to get more creative with our guest lists. You may read the words *crippled* and *lame* and think they sound like old-fashioned Bible words. In actuality, there are those all around us with physical limitations. Their eyes, ears, or legs that don't work properly do not make them any different on the inside.

Expanding our guest lists requires us to consider others, not just ourselves. Reaching out to someone who looks or seems a bit different from you will feel good. Likely you will notice that you have more in common than you'd imagined.

There is certainly reward in heaven for believers who demonstrate this type of kindness. The reward on earth is sweet as well. It may provide you with an unexpected new friend.

EMILY BIGGERS
DAILY ENCOURAGEMENT FOR SINGLE WOMEN

The Power of Connection

A friend loves at all times.

PROVERBS 17:17 NIV

What would we do without friends? They encourage and inspire us. They listen as if they really care—because they do. Good friends seek to understand and empathize with us. Even when they can't relate, they care about us anyway.

Like snowflakes, no two friendships are the same; each brings a unique beauty and joy to our lives. We have acquaintances, casual friends, close friends, and "heart" friends, that handful of women with whom we share our deepest selves. Jesus had different circles of friends, too. He ministered to the crowds, He spent significant time with the twelve disciples, and He was closest to three men: Peter, James, and John. He was companion to tax collectors and sinners (Mark 2:15–17), as well as to His dearly loved friends Mary, Martha, and Lazarus (John 11:20–32).

Today each of us can have the joy of knowing Jesus as our friend (John 15:15). In the quiet solitude of prayer, we can pour out our deepest fears and desires. We can take pleasure in enjoying God—in just being in His company.

When we fellowship with God in prayer, we can then pray powerfully for our earthly friends. We can pray *for* them and *with* them in Jesus' name.

That's perhaps one of the best ways we can show a friend we care. Maybe we should stop to thank God for the wonderful women in our lives—those women who've given us the gift of friendship—and ask Him how we can be a better friend to others.

JACKIE M. JOHNSON
POWER PRAYERS FOR WOMEN

Choose Your Friends Carefully

My son, if sinners entice thee, consent thou not.
PROVERBS 1:10 KJV

My dear friend, choose your friends carefully, and keep them loyal. While you are kind to those who have fallen, remember that it is not for you, a young girl, to raise them up by seeking their company. You are too easily drawn away yourself. Let your friends be chosen from among those whom you can admire and emulate, that is, those whose conversation and deportment will lead you up instead of down. Keep in mind, of course, the two classes of friends, that outward group to whom you are always sociable and friendly and the inner group with whom you become really intimate. One should be friends with those who need friendship even if they are not so desirable, but no girl can become intimate with people of low standards

and morals without becoming contaminated. If you are
a young Christian, seek out friends among those who are
longer in the service and keep out of the company of those
who draw your mind away from things that are right.

MABEL HALE
BEAUTIFUL GIRLHOOD

Overcoming Shyness

*He said to them, "Do you bring in a lamp
to put it under a bowl or a bed?
Instead, don't you put it on its stand?"*

MARK 4:21 NIV

You keep to yourself, not going out of your way to
risk friendship with anybody. They've hurt you, and you
aren't going to let them ever do it again. I know the pain
is unbearable and sometimes you don't want to go on,
but there is a way around it, a way through it. Follow me
close here: People will treat you the way you expect to be
treated. If you expect people to be friendly and treat you
well, you just may find that they are willing to do that if
you give them a chance.

I know it's hard to be shy, believe me, but I also
know that you can overcome your shy tendencies with
a little effort and faith. All my life I have been terribly

shy. I feel weak in large groups. I am at a loss for words. I am uncomfortable and scared. But I know that God is stronger than all that, and I know that He calls me to love my neighbor, so I do what I can do to care for people. People are shocked to hear that I'm shy when they see me speaking in front of twenty thousand women and talking to thousands of them one-on-one through my book lines, but I can do it only because I trust God and know He will give me the words. You can do it, too. I believe in you. You can find ways to cover up your shyness and obey God's Word in the face of your fear.

HAYLEY DIMARCO
MEAN GIRLS ALL GROWN UP

Iron-Sharpening Friendship

*As iron sharpens iron, so a man sharpens
the countenance of his friend.*

PROVERBS 27:17 NKJV

Maybe you're familiar with the biblical expression "iron sharpens iron." But what does it mean? In order to keep things like knives sharp, they have to be rubbed against something equally as hard—something that can shape them into effective tools.

Godly friends will sharpen us. They won't let us grow dull in our relationship with God or with others. They will keep us on our toes and will work with the Lord to shape us into the most effective people we can be. Rubbing against them won't always be fun. In fact, we might feel the friction at times and wish we could run in the opposite direction. But don't run! Allow God to do the work He longs to do.

Take a good look at the friends God has placed in your life. Are there some who don't sharpen you? Perhaps you've been put in their lives to sharpen them. Are there a few who diligently participate in your life, growing you into a better, stronger person? Do they rub you the wrong way at times? Praise God! He's shaping and sharpening you into the person you are meant to be.

JANICE HANNA
DAILY ENCOURAGEMENT FOR SINGLE WOMEN

Friendly Love

I thank my God upon every remembrance of you,
always in every prayer of mine for you all
making request with joy.

PHILIPPIANS 1:3–4 KJV

Have you worked with some wonderful people? You spend so much time on the job, chances are that you've made some work friendships. Maybe you rarely see these folks outside of work, but they still hold a treasured place in your heart.

If a coworker moves on to a new job, relocates to another state, or retires, those fond memories remain with you. As you look back, you may feel thankful, as Paul did when he thought of the Philippian church. But do you also thank God and pray for that person?

As a caring Christian who believes God can work

through prayer, even when people are far distant, why not lift a special workplace friend up to Him? Thank Him for that friendship. If you still keep in touch, pray specifically for that friend's joys and needs. Even if you don't see each other, always pray for his or her well-being.

You may not see your friend this side of heaven, but when you meet again in eternity, the blessings of those prayers will touch you both.

PAMELA L. MCQUADE
DAILY WISDOM FOR THE WORKPLACE

Easily Improve Your Relationships

And pray in the Spirit on all occasions with all kinds of prayers and requests. With this in mind, be alert and always keep on praying for all the Lord's people.

EPHESIANS 6:18 NIV

When you pray for anyone you tend to modify your personal attitude toward him. You thereby lift the relationship to a higher level" (Norman Vincent Peale). One of the most practical steps you can take to improve any relationship is simply to begin praying for the other person. It is almost impossible to remain angry, bitter, or indifferent toward someone when you are actively praying for his or her welfare. It is difficult to treat someone cruelly while asking God to bring about the best in his or her life. And it is much easier to forgive an offense as you pray for someone and begin to see that person broken at the foot of the cross—or in need of a Savior.

Begin praying for everyone you meet. Even total strangers! One way to move people from your list of acquaintances to your list of friends is to inquire how you can pray for them. Then pray for them each day, asking for updates on a routine basis. Soon you will know this person's nearest concerns and they will know you truly care!

DONNA PARTOW
BECOMING THE WOMAN I WANT TO BE

Wisdom Comes from God

He came to His hometown and began teaching them in their synagogue, so that they were astonished, and said, "Where did this man get this wisdom and these miraculous powers?"

MATTHEW 13:54 NASB

The toughest critics you'll ever encounter are family and friends. The reason is simple: They know you best. When vulnerability swings your trapeze with such speed that your grip loosens, they watch as you fall. At that moment you can stand there gazing at your flattened imprint in the dirt or climb up the ladder and try again.

Yes, some will continue to stare, waiting for you to stumble once again, but there will be new faces in your crowd of onlookers. They believe you can reach your goals and make a difference in our world. They do not see a little girl living next door; they see you as you are *now*.

Jesus encountered these same narrow-minded pessimists, those who claimed they knew Him from way back. Ridiculing Him, they said, "Isn't He just a carpenter's son?" Yes, He surely was, but that carpenter was the Master Builder! For Jesus wasn't Joseph's son, but God's Son.

He came from God, full of wisdom. Those who stood with Him during His earthly ministry had true wisdom and understanding from God. They made up His true family of believers. Today, you obtain wisdom through a personal knowledge of Christ and by studying His Word. For only then can God's Spirit fill you with the wisdom you'll need to find and live out your God-given purpose.

CAROL L. FITZPATRICK
DAILY WISDOM FOR WOMEN

God's Friend

"But you, O Israel, my servant, Jacob, whom I have chosen, you descendants of Abraham my friend, I took you from the ends of the earth, from its farthest corners I called you. I said, "You are my servant"; I have chosen you and have not rejected you."

Isaiah 41: 8-9

Have you pondered the idea that, like Israel, the Lord of the universe is your friend? Perhaps you've been stopped in your tracks by the awe of that truth. *Why should He care for me?* you may wonder.

God chooses His friends on His own terms. The famous, the extraordinarily intelligent, the powerful aren't always on His list. Yet some of the most unexpected folks are. He doesn't choose based on worldly greatness (He doesn't need it, because He has enough greatness of His own). His own sense of mercy defines the choice, in ways we cannot now understand.

Many blessings follow friendship with God, but so

do challenges. The Creator expects much of His friends, just as He gives much. He doesn't ask just anyone to take on the job, which also requires training in faithfulness. Anyone not willing to do His will need not apply for the position. Being a friend of Jesus requires that we suffer, struggle, and face numerous challenges, physically and spiritually. It's not the kind of thing He offers lightly or we should accept blindly.

But when God chooses a friend, it's forever. He never gives up or changes His mind. He's with you for this lifetime and eternity. Along with all the purely delightful things in His hand, He offers strength in trials and guidance for a long, hard way. Nothing that happens is beyond His strength or help.

That's the best friendship anyone could offer.

Pamela McQuade
Daily Wisdom to Satisfy the Soul

I Am a Friend of God

When Jesus saw their faith, he said,
"Friend, your sins are forgiven."

LUKE 5:20 NIV

Friendships are critical to women, and godly friendships are the best. Can you even imagine a world without your girlfriends in it? Impossible! Who would you share your hopes and dreams with? Your goals and aspirations? Oh, what a blessing women of God are! They breathe hope and life into us when we need it most. They laugh along with us at chick flicks. They cry with us when our hearts are broken.

Isn't it amazing to realize God calls us His friend? He reaches out to us with a friendship that goes above and beyond the very best the world has to offer. Best of all, He's not the sort of friend who loses touch or forgets to call.

He's always there. And while your earthly friends might do a good job of comforting you when you're down, their brand of comfort doesn't even begin to compare with the Lord's. He knows just what to say when things go wrong, and knows how to throw an amazing celebration when things go well for you.

Today, thank the Lord—not just for salvation, not just for the work He's done in your heart, not just for the people and things He's placed in your life—but for calling you His friend.

JANICE HANNA
DAILY ENCOURAGEMENT FOR SINGLE WOMEN

Walk and Pray

Pray in the Spirit at all times and on every occasion.
Stay alert and be persistent in your prayers
for all believers everywhere.

EPHESIANS 6:18 NLT

Their friendship began when their daughters played on the same soccer team. Leaning against their cars, they chatted and waited for practice to end, both realizing after a couple of conversations that they had more in common than two energetic thirteen-year-old girls. They shared a common faith in God, and both women were experiencing the growing pains that come with parenting adolescents.

One day the women decided to start wearing their workout gear to practice so that they could talk and pray for their daughters as they walked the perimeter of the soccer field. By the end of the season, both women were encouraged and strengthened, and they had forged a deep friendship. The added bonus was their increased fitness levels derived from these long walks.

Jesus said, "For where two or three come together in my name, there am I with them" (Matthew 18:20 NIV). Real power is available when friends get together for fellowship and prayer, because Christ Himself is right there with them. Along with gaining another's insight and perspective, anytime we share a burden with a friend, our load instantly becomes lighter.

Is there a friend you might call today to join you in a prayer walk?

AUSTINE KELLER
WHISPERS OF WISDOM FOR BUSY WOMEN

A Winning Look

No, in all these things we are more
than conquerors through him who loved us.

ROMANS 8:37 NIV

Ahh. . .the dreaded last word. Are you a gotta-have-the-last-word kind of gal? Do you always have to be right? When you always have to be right, people tend to shy away from you. They will conveniently have an excuse "not to see you" every time you want to get together. And can we blame them? What our mothers used to tell us is really true—pretty is as pretty does. If you act ugly, people will view you as ugly, and they won't want to be around you.

So if we know that having to have the last word makes us unattractive, why do we continue in this behavior? Because we are taught that winning is everything. We're taught, "Nice guys (and gals) finish last." But those teachings are directly opposed to the Word of God.

Don't get me wrong—Jesus is all about winning, but not at someone else's expense. He wants us to succeed, but He wants us to do it His way. When we do it His way, we'll still have friends when we arrive at that all-important winner's circle.

So stop looking out for "number one" and start looking to *the* One! Let Him mold you into the beautiful creature He's created you to be! Realize that you don't have to get the last word in. His Word is word enough. And begin following in Jesus' footsteps. His steps always lead to victory, and you'll look good on the journey!

MICHELLE MEDLOCK ADAMS
SECRETS OF BEAUTY

Keeping in Touch

Having many things to write unto you, I would not write with paper and ink: but I trust to come unto you, and speak face to face, that our joy may be full.

2 JOHN 12 KJV

Some people have had a powerful impact on your career. A mentor has shown you the ropes, but you've moved on from that first job, and you hardly keep in touch anymore. It's not that you don't care, but life gets in the way. Or perhaps one of you moved miles away, and keeping in touch is difficult.

John knew what separation from loved ones was like. He'd probably taught this "elect lady" (v. 1 KJV) whom he wrote to, and she and her family had won a place in his heart. Being apart made communication difficult, and perhaps John was nervous about putting his thoughts on paper, since this letter was likely to be read publicly and word would be passed on to the deceivers who were undoubtedly impacting the lady's church (v. 7).

John had to travel many miles to see the lady again. Though you might like to visit your friend, travel is not your only option. Drop her an e-mail. Pick up a phone and give him a call. You may not speak face-to-face, but the communion you have can still make your joy full.

PAMELA L. McQUADE
DAILY WISDOM FOR THE WORKPLACE

Cultivating Positivity

Walk with the wise and become wise,
for a companion of fools suffers harm.

PROVERBS 13:20 NIV

Are you living in a destructive relationship? If you are trying to recover from emotional damage. . . , you need to protect yourself from having to swim through someone else's bondage. Cultivate positive, uplifting relationships.

This is not a license to run every time someone challenges or confronts you. But if you step back from the relationship, your objectivity will return, and you will be able to tell if the person is confronting in love or attacking with a spirit of criticism and control. Remember, laying down your life for another doesn't mean allowing the person to run over you. Ask God about any relationship that destroys the joy of life in you, and pray for Him to show you what you should do. If you can't leave this person, ask God to help you confront him. Ask Him to change both of you; then take the steps necessary to see restoration happen.

The Lord may ask you to lay down your life for a relationship. You let a part of you die so that something greater will be made alive. You will *know* when God is asking you to do that. You will *choose* to do it; it won't be inflicted on you. You will feel peace, not anguish. Until a time like that, examine any relationship that brings out the worst in you. Don't allow yourself to be battered— physically, mentally, or emotionally.

STORMIE OMARTIAN
FINDING PEACE FOR YOUR HEART

The Blessing of Friendship

Two people are better off than one,
for they can help each other succeed.
If one person falls, the other can reach out and help.
But someone who falls alone is in real trouble.

ECCLESIASTES 4:9–10 NLT

Two friends sat in a doctor's office waiting for one of the ladies' test results. The doctor entered the room in a white lab coat, carrying a clipboard. On the clipboard were papers filled with numbers representing hormone levels and blood cell counts that could only be deciphered by a trained eye. Before the doctor spoke, she asked her patient if it was okay to deliver the news in front of the woman waiting with her. "Yes, of course, Doctor," the patient replied. "This is my *friend*."

Life is filled with surprises, some wonderful but others

horrifying. A loved one dies. A spouse leaves. An employer treats us unjustly. We face breakups and breakdowns, full schedules and empty nests. Life is much easier with a friend.

Do you have a friend who is, as Proverbs 18:24 states, closer than a brother? If you have not cultivated this type of friendship, pray that God might lead you as you seek to do so. If you have a close friend, thank the Lord for her today.

All of us stumble in life. Occasionally we even fall down. What a blessing it is to have a friend to help us up!

EMILY BIGGERS
WHISPERS OF WISDOM FOR BUSY WOMEN

God's Gift Bearers

God has given each of you a gift from his great variety of spiritual gifts. Use them well to serve one another.

1 Peter 4:10 NLT

We don't know what is going on in the lives of those we brush shoulders with every day. Only God can give us eyes to see and ears to hear and the grace to be the fragrance of Christ where life has turned sour. Often, those who have experienced a terrible loss have the added wound of feeling as if they have suddenly become a social pariah and people are avoiding them. It's hard to know what to do or say when we meet someone who has gone through a great tragedy. I have discovered that there is no right thing to say, but we can always give ourselves. At times a warm embrace, a shared silent moment, or a few shed tears means more than eloquent words.

It may seem strange to talk about such painful issues in a book on [friendship], but I believe there is a mystery at work here. When Adam and Eve walked with God in the garden, one of the hallmarks of their lives was oneness with each other and God. Satan's nature then and now is to bring division and isolation, to make men, women, and children carry their burdens alone. We are invited to be part of God's antidote to that demonic poison and reach out with the love and compassion of Christ.

We have the joy of inviting the Holy Spirit to empower us to be gift bearers, to embrace the lonely, wounded ones with the heart of our Father.

SHEILA WALSH
CONTAGIOUS JOY

Friends Bring Happiness

Friends love through all kinds of weather.

PROVERBS 17:17 MSG

Television shows, hit songs, and countless stories have focused on the special people we call friends. Special occasions such as "Friendship Week" and "Best Friend Day" have even been established to honor them. Why? Because friends are important.

Friends are there for us in good times and bad. They support us when we need a shoulder to cry on. They encourage us when we need a boost of confidence. They celebrate with us when we accomplish our goals. They offer words of wisdom when we need advice. And, maybe most important, friends make life's journey a whole lot happier.

Do you have special friends in your life? If so, how long has it been since you have taken time to get together with them, phone them, or drop them a card to say hello? Friendships take work. They require a time investment on your part. But they are definitely worth the time and effort.

If you don't have any close friends with whom you can share your life, ask God to send you some of those precious people. Or if you have been neglecting your friends, determine today to rekindle those relationships.

God didn't intend for us to go through life alone. He knew we would need each other. He knew that friends would add a dimension of happiness to our lives that we wouldn't be able to get anywhere else. So celebrate your friends today—and enjoy the journey of life a little bit more.

MICHELLE MEDLOCK ADAMS
SECRETS OF HAPPINESS

Framed Love

"Love your neighbor as yourself."

MARK 12:31 NIV

Dwarfing all of life's sorrows, framed in my memory are countless pictures of love. Early on, there's a picture of my mother making a second birthday cake and party after mumps ruined the first one. Another followed shortly afterward when I had pneumonia and our furnace quit on an icy winter night. My mother built a roaring fire in the fireplace and dragged the couch in front of it for me to sleep.

I remember my Aunt Char's kitchen with its cup of silver spoons on the table where she regularly served Mother, my brother Roger, and me tea with homemade cookies after school, listening with smiles and interest to our day's events. Her Bible stories in Sunday school stayed with me for years.

But seldom have I experienced the love of Christ more than in one framed memory of four of my dear friends calling themselves "The Love Squad," who invaded our home during a painful hospital vigil and restored it to beauty and order, filled every room with flowers, left gifts on each clean bed, and meals in the oven and the freezer. I keep these memories as treasures in my heart, taking them out and fingering them often with gratefulness.

How many framed love stories do you have? As you remember them, thank God for each one. He was the Source all along.

VIRELLE KIDDER
MEET ME AT THE WELL

Fellowship

If we live in the light, as God is in the light,
we can share fellowship with each other.

1 John 1:7 ncv

The word *fellowship* sounded strange and "churchy"
when I first heard it. It reminded me of tea and cookies
after a missionary meeting or a potluck dinner in
the church basement. I've since discovered it's much
more than just coffee hour. Its dictionary definition is
"companionship, a friendly association, mutual sharing,
a group of people with the same interests." In the biblical
sense, it's even more than that. "Fellowship has to do with
a mutuality in all parts of your life," [my pastor] taught
us. "You bear one another's burdens and fulfill the law of
Christ. You pray for one another, you love one another,
you help one another when there is material need, you

weep with those who weep and rejoice with those who rejoice. It's growing in an association with people who are moving in the same pathway you are and sharing with each other in your times of victory or need or your times of trial or triumph. It's growing in relationship."

Fellowship is instrumental in shaping us. The Bible says that we become like those we spend time with and good friends sharpen one another just as iron sharpens iron (Proverbs 27:17). This is reason enough to spend time with other believers, but there is even more to it. . . . Certain visitations of God's power happen only in the midst of. . .gatherings of believers. Make it a point to be a part of that.

STORMIE OMARTIAN
FINDING PEACE FOR YOUR HEART

How to Know If You're in Love

If I speak with the tongues of men and of angels,
but do not have love, I have become
a noisy gong or a clanging cymbal.

1 Corinthians 13:1 nasb

Although we love each other deeply, I know there will be times when we'll fail to be there for one another. That's when we'll go to the Lord to receive in abundance what we lack." These words of wisdom were spoken by a twenty-four-year-old woman who had just become engaged. If only more marriages began this way! For even though we've prayed for godly mates, and then relied on His guidance, there will still be times when our attempts to love are less than perfect.

However, if both man and woman turn back to God's blueprint, harmony can be restored. "Love is patient, love is kind and is not jealous; love does not brag and is not arrogant, does not act unbecomingly; it does not seek its own, is not provoked, does not take into account a wrong suffered, does not rejoice in unrighteousness, but rejoices with the truth; bears all things, believes all things, hopes all things, endures all things. Love never fails" (1 Corinthians 13:4–8 NASB).

Why don't more people tap into this resource? To truly love someone means that we will always place that person's welfare above our own. This, after all, is how God loves us.

CAROL L. FITZPATRICK
DAILY WISDOM FOR WOMEN

Sharing God's Truth

I came to you in weakness
with great fear and trembling.

1 CORINTHIANS 2:3 NIV

Do you know who wrote these words? Paul. That great preacher, the one who almost single-handedly reached the Western world, came to the Corinthians in fear and trembling. Can you imagine this man, whose signature is on so much of the New Testament, being afraid of telling people about Jesus? It hardly seems possible.

It's not uncommon for Christians to experience fear when they talk about Jesus. Bill Bright, leader of Campus Crusade for many years, admitted that witnessing did not come easily to him. He told his staff that he did it because God had commanded it.

But in the next verse, 1 Corinthians 2:4, Paul tells how

he managed to overcome his fear. He spoke not in his own power, but in the power of the Holy Spirit. He explains that he did not want listeners' faith to rest on men's wisdom, but on God's.

Today, are you afraid to share your faith or take a stand for what is right? Don't stand in your own strength, but in God's. Ask the Spirit to guide you, and speak as He directs.

PAMELA L. McQUADE
DAILY WISDOM FOR THE WORKPLACE

Take It from the Dogs

A merry heart maketh a cheerful countenance:
but by sorrow of the heart the spirit is broken.

PROVERBS 15:13 KJV

You know that silly grin on most dogs' faces? A good many dogs appear to find life quite entertaining, and why not? They don't have a care in the world. Their meals are served to them in personalized dishes. They have nice warm beds or at least straw-lined doghouses where they spend their time dreaming of chasing cars, tormenting less vicious creatures, or having their bellies rubbed. Ahh, the privileged lives they lead.

Typically when a person approaches a dog, he can determine pretty quickly how the dog feels about his presence. There's the telltale wag of the tail and excited pant that says the dog was just waiting for someone to welcome. On the other hand, some dogs will greet you with a snarl and a snap of the jaws that lets you know you are quite possibly overstepping your bounds. Likewise, the expression on a person's face often tells very much about her. A person with a happy expression is generally more pleasant to be around than someone with a sour look, because what's on your face reflects what's in your soul.

Did you know that the average child laughs 150 times each day? The average adult is closer to 15. Why is this? Well, in general, adults do have more to be concerned about than children do, but that sounds like more of an excuse than a reason. Perhaps we need to practice laughing more until it becomes second nature. Read a joke book; watch a funny movie; play a crazy game. Watch silly kids— or silly animals. Enjoy the humor God has blessed you with. Your friends—furry and not—will thank you.

RACHEL QUILLIN
HEAVENLY HUMOR FOR THE DOG LOVER'S SOUL

Lonely People

"Never will I leave you; never will I forsake you."

HEBREWS 13:5 NIV

Sir Francis Bacon said, "A crowd is not company, and faces are but a gallery of pictures, and talk but a tinkling cymbal, where there is no love." Whether you're one of the 90 million singles in America or in a marriage vacant of loving communications, you're no doubt well acquainted with the emotional pain of loneliness.

Loneliness is that feeling of isolation and emptiness. It's that deep feeling of being separated, cut off, and disconnected from others and can happen behind closed doors in the solitude of one's home or in a crowd.

Take Kate for example. She's confident, charismatic, witty, and single. She travels frequently with her job and knows lots of people. The truth is her many acquaintances are just that—acquaintances. She has no real meaningful relationships outside of work. But there is something she and you can do to turn things around.

Get connected. Learn how to become a good friend so you can find a good friend. Also, look for ways to help someone else. It's been said that loneliness is "the only disease that can be cured by adding two or more cases together." By helping others, you not only attend to your own aloneness but also meet the relational needs of someone else.

Finally, practice the presence of God and look for "God sightings" throughout the day. After all, He said He'd never leave or forsake you!

BOBBIE RILL
FAMILY LIFE RADIO NETWORK

Handling Loneliness with Grace

I am not alone, for my Father is with me.

JOHN 16:32 NIV

Loneliness feels like trying to waltz without a partner....

Many of us seek solace in the refrigerator. We try to drown our lonesomeness in a friendly jug of caramel Frappuccino with a Blizzard chaser. We companion ourselves by getting up close and personal with a vat full of cheese sauce–slathered pasta. But instead of relieving isolation, we end up feeling not only lonesome but also loathsome. Even dancing alone becomes too challenging with the added tonnage weighing down our self-esteem.

Others of us try to cover our personal agony by talking too loud, too much, or not at all. Hiding in silence is a real door-closer to relationships. Some become braggarts, name-droppers, comediennes, and storytellers—as in whoppers. Others of us shop too much, work too much, sleep too much, or just plain do too much....

So what's the solution? For me, it helps to understand that loneliness is part of the human package and that connecting with others is vital for my well-being. Sometimes another person is just what the doctor ordered; at other times, people can be our greatest pain and the reason we need a doctor. . .of psychology.

Realizing that other folks weren't designed to be the final answer for our struggle with isolation keeps us from blaming them for our condition and protects them and us from unfair expectations. Friendships work much better when you understand what a person can and can't bring to the girlfriend party.

PATSY CLAIRMONT
DANCING BONES

Simply Irresistible

Love never fails.

1 Corinthians 13:8 niv

*I*f you found out you could become simply irresistible, wouldn't you want to know how? If the ability to become irresistible came in a bottle, wouldn't you rush to the store to buy it? You probably would, because people from all walks of life would love to know that secret.

The advertising executives know this, which is why they call perfumes "Very Irresistible" and other similar names. These advertising executives know women desire that irresistible quality and that they'll pay almost anything to achieve it.

Well, search no more. I have the secret to being irresistible, and you can't get it in a bottle or a potion of any kind. You'll only find it in the Bible. God's love is what makes us irresistible. The more you have on the inside of you, the more irresistible you'll become.

See, people are drawn to the love of God. They long for it. God made us that way—with a void inside that can only be filled and satisfied with His love. Here's some additional good news: God's love never fails. Open God's Word and read 1 Corinthians 13 today, and ask the Lord to fill you with His love. Soon, you'll be absolutely irresistible.

MICHELLE MEDLOCK ADAMS
SECRETS OF BEAUTY

To Follow Those Who Teach Us

But Ruth said, "Do not urge me to leave you
or turn back from following you; for where you go,
I will go, and where you lodge, I will lodge.
Your people shall be my people, and your God, my God."

RUTH 1:16 NASB

Ruth must have been frightened. With the loss of both her husband and brother-in-law, and the death of her father-in-law years earlier, Ruth's future was uncertain. Tradition said she should return to her parents' home, but Ruth and her sister-in-law, Orpah, clustered around Naomi, the grieving mother of their husbands. Ruth didn't want to return to her father's house, but three widows had no way of supporting themselves.

Then Ruth's beloved mother-in-law, Naomi, decided to return to Judah. Naomi had family in Judah who could take care of her, and as she prepared to move, Ruth and Orpah faced a decision.

Although Orpah loved Naomi, she recognized the wisdom in Naomi's advice, "Return, my daughters. Why should you go with me?" (Ruth 1:11 NASB). Ruth, however, had a dilemma that went beyond financial support. Her closeness to Naomi, and the spiritual devotion of their home, had led Ruth to love the Lord. Ruth chose to trust God and the wisdom of Naomi. She placed herself in their care, and when Naomi instructed her on how to win the affection of Boaz, Ruth followed her guidance. Her trust resulted in a secure home and an honored place in the genealogy of Christ.

As women, we benefit from the wisdom of our sisters. Trusting God and choosing a wise mentor can help us as we develop a deeper relationship with our Lord.

RAMONA RICHARDS
SECRETS OF CONFIDENCE

The Power of Active Faith

Faith by itself, if it is not accompanied by action, is dead.
JAMES 2:17 NIV

Everyone has their own spiritual gift they can use to serve or minister to others.

Feeling as if you're not "holy" enough to serve others? Relax. You are *already* holy and sanctified because you have faith in Jesus Christ and have accepted Him as your Savior. Through Christ, God created you and set you apart to do good works.

So it appears there is no excuse for not serving God. Perhaps the problem is that we are not sure what God has called us to do. Not even Paul was certain as to his role in God's plan. "What shall I do, Lord?" he asked. And God answered, "Get up. . .and go into Damascus. There you will be told all that you have been assigned to do."

God has an assignment for each and every one of us. All we have to do is ask Him where and how He would like us to serve. Our gifts need not be limited to those listed in 1 Corinthians 12:8–10. The Church also needs those gifted in writing, music, hospitality, teaching, preaching, intercessory prayer, and missions, to name a few.

God doesn't want you just sitting in the pew every Sunday as you watch others ministering to your needs. According to His plan, although you are important to Him, it's not all about *you*. It's all about *God*.

Find your spiritual gifts, ones that you love to use, so that you will be filled with a passion to serve. And then use them to God's great glory.

DONNA K. MALTESE
POWER PRAYERS TO START YOUR DAY

Working for a Friend

A friend loveth at all times,
and a brother is born for adversity.

PROVERBS 17:17 KJV

If your boss is also your friend, count yourself blessed. But also accept that at times she's going to make decisions you'll wish she hadn't made. Though you agree in many things, there will be some choices you would have made differently, for whatever reason. Those differences of opinion could destroy your friendship, if you let them.

But if you recognize that she has the position of authority and accept that, your friendship can stand firm. After all, if you were the boss, you'd get to make the decisions, but if you were wrong, you'd also get the flak. She makes her own choices and stands firm in them. If she makes a mistake, it's her responsibility, not yours.

If you truly are your boss's friend, you'll recognize that even people who disagree on some things can remain friends. You'll give her the kind of leeway you'd give a friend whose taste in clothes you don't always agree on or who doesn't make the wisest choices in her romantic life. Though you might offer a suggestion on occasion, you won't take every different decision as a personal affront.

Love your friend faithfully, no matter what her position.

PAMELA L. McQUADE
DAILY WISDOM FOR THE WORKPLACE

Moving Day

Perfume and incense bring joy to the heart,
and the pleasantness of a friend
springs from their heartfelt advice.

PROVERBS 27:9 NIV

When I made the decision to leave California and head for Texas, I was inundated with offers from friends and even strangers to help.

Can I bring lunch? Can I help you pack? Can I drive with you to Texas? Can I feed your dog? Well, I didn't have a dog, but had I, somebody would have offered to feed him. When I got here, Texas was just as gracious in her welcome as California had been in her farewell. My Texas buddies and I watched my house go up in fits and spurts. We prayed over the foundation, walls, roof, and yard. We pooled our resources of time and money as some folks planned on-site picnics while others brought Starbucks and brownies.

The day it was time for my furniture to leave its storage place and waltz in the door, I had so many helpers they almost had to wear name tags. I even had matching black T-shirts made with a white logo reading "Team Luci." My friends proved that now-famous Home Depot motto: "You can do it. We can help." They epitomized the Golden Rule of Scripture: "Do to others as you would have them do to you" (Luke 6:31 NIV). When everybody pitches in, the world seems like a better place and the work is a lot more fun, don't you think? Teamwork! A God-given concept.

I actually moved in on Labor Day. I signed all the papers thirty days before, but because of the warmth and love of the friends with whom I was staying, they encouraged me to take my time to settle in. "Keep the new house as your 'project,' Luci, but don't move in until you're ready." So I did exactly that. I loved that lingering spirit of acceptance and camaraderie.

LUCI SWINDOLL
CONTAGIOUS JOY

Untamed Words

*Jesus called the crowd to him and said,
"Listen and understand. What goes into your mouth does not
defile you, but what comes out of your mouth,
that is what defiles you."*

MATTHEW 15:10–11 NIV

Words coming out of our mouths are far more serious than donuts going in. Donuts aren't good for you and, yes, they put on pounds, but they won't kill you. Untamed words, however, can poison relationships, destroy marriage, slay fragile hearts, smear the image of God, and weaken others' faith. The power of words lasts for eternity. How have others' words affected you? Are there some that still sting since childhood? Or last night?

Wouldn't you love to become the complete opposite: a woman whose whole person reflects the tenderness of

Christ? I would. What a difference that would make to those in our world. When our thoughts, our wills, our worship are permeated more and more with Christ, His words find a willing partner in our tongues, our eyes, our talents, and our energies. It's as natural as a hand in a glove. Jesus fills us, His heart in ours, His thoughts finding expression in our voices, His energy creating love in motion in our world. What a miracle!

Satan can't imitate that. No one can for long. As soon as we are disturbed, the truth will spill out for all to see and hear. A person's tongue reveals what's inside the mind and announces who runs the ship.

VIRELLE KIDDER
MEET ME AT THE WELL

Nobody's Perfect

God keeps an eye on his friends,
his ears pick up every moan and groan.

PSALM 34:15 MSG

There is also strength in being with believers *outside* the church. When you make friends with people who follow the Lord, there is a strong bond of love that makes other relationships seem shallow. Such friendships are the most fulfilling and healing. They can also be the most frustrating because we expect *Christians* to be perfect when in reality only *Christ* is perfect.

It's helpful to think of all fellowship with believers as beneficial: the pleasant encounters are *healing* and the unpleasant ones are *stretching*. When you run across believers who stretch you more than you feel you can handle, don't turn away from God. Remember He is still perfect and good even if some of His children aren't. God always loves and respects you, even if a few of His offspring don't. I know that nothing hurts worse than a wound inflicted by a brother or sister in the Lord. Having been wounded many times like that myself, I am forced to remember that we will be imperfect until we go to be with Jesus. So we need to be merciful to those who "stretch" us and forgive quickly. Besides, we are probably stretching others ourselves.

STORMIE OMARTIAN
FINDING PEACE FOR YOUR HEART

Perfect Friends

But if we walk in the light, as he is in the light,
we have fellowship with one another,
and the blood of Jesus, his Son, purifies us from all sin.

1 JOHN 1:7 NIV

Imagine living in a perfect, problem-free world—where there is no crime, no traffic jams, no pollution, no disease, and no war! Imagine feeling really, really good physically and emotionally—having no hang-ups, no headaches, no regrets, no unwanted cellulite, no struggle with depression or anxiety, and no guilt! Imagine having a perfect friend who totally loved you and with whom you could communicate freely without fear of being misunderstood.

That's what Adam and Eve experienced with God and each other in the Garden of Eden. And yet, even under those perfect circumstances, they blew it. Adam and Eve made decisions that led to the deterioration of those perfect relationships.

You've no doubt blown it, too. Maybe you said something or did something you've come to regret that has broken trust, caused a relationship to end, and left you alone and feeling ashamed. God's got you covered!

In Genesis 3:21, God made Adam and Eve the first handcrafted, designer garments to cover the shame of their sin. And He demonstrated His incomparable love for them and you through the life and death of His perfect Son, Jesus. Jesus is the One who has paved the way to restoration—restoration with God Himself, which also impacts your relationships with others. You don't live in a perfect world, but you can be in perfect relationship with God.

BOBBIE RILL
FAMILY LIFE RADIO NETWORK

A Surprise in the Closet

*"So in everything, do to others what
you would have them do to you."*

MATTHEW 7:12 NIV

Ugh! I tried pushing the hangers in my bedroom closet. Curling my fingers behind the metal rod, I felt the obstacle preventing my success. I pulled out a wad—it was crumpled ten-dollar bills!

I rushed to the phone and called my husband. "You'll never guess what just happened! I found $800 in our closet!" Tom was as stunned as I was.

Seven years earlier we had purchased our home from a man named Fred. Fred's daughter, Judy, lived in our subdivision. I struggled with whether the money should go to Judy. The following Sunday I felt like a bolt of lightning hit me. God spoke to my heart saying, *Go! Go now!*

When Judy opened the door, I could see she had been crying. She graciously invited me inside.

"Judy, a couple of weeks ago while I was moving the clothes in my closet, I discovered some money hidden up under the rod."

Dropping her head, she smiled. "That would have been my mother."

"Well, this money belongs to you."

Tears streamed down her face. "I was missing my mother so badly. I said aloud to God, 'Please, just let me know my mom is okay.' Then you showed up at the door."

God was there, waiting to answer her call.

SHARI MINKE
KISSES OF SUNSHINE FOR WOMEN

Be Humble, Admit Mistakes

"Pick me up and throw me into the sea," he replied,
"and it will become calm. I know that it is my fault
that this great storm has come upon you."

JONAH 1:12 NIV

Jonah knew he'd made a mistake before he even hit land. Out in the middle of the sea, while he was traveling to Tarshish, a storm hit. When the other passengers on the ship cast lots and discovered he was the cause of their trouble, the prophet immediately admitted to it. Jonah was bighearted enough to be willing to have them toss him into the sea just to save the vessel.

When we make mistakes, are we quickly willing to do whatever it takes to make them right? Jonah might not have wanted to go to Nineveh, but neither did he want his disobedience to cost the lives of his fellow travelers. He took responsibility for the wrong and found a way to fix it, even at the cost of his own life.

Everyone makes mistakes on the job, but not many are brave enough to admit them. That doesn't mean the boss can't figure it out, just that it takes a little more time or effort. Admit to your mistakes, and maybe, like Jonah, you'll find that your coworkers aren't in a rush to slip you over the side.

PAMELA L. McQUADE
DAILY WISDOM FOR THE WORKPLACE

Turn and Strengthen Your Brothers

"Simon, Simon, Satan has asked to sift all of you as wheat. But I have prayed for you, Simon, that your faith may not fail. And when you have turned back, strengthen your brothers."

LUKE 22:31–32 NIV

Did Jesus promise to stop Satan from picking on Peter? No. Did He say He would prevent Peter from failing? No. Did He tell Peter nothing bad would ever happen to him? No. Quite the contrary. Jesus said, in essence, "You're going to be tested beyond your limits, and you're going to blow it big-time. Then you'll probably spend some time beating yourself up about it. But when you're done wallowing in regret, get up and use it for good."

Isn't it amazing that Jesus handpicked Peter, knowing full well in advance every mistake He would ever make?

Why? Because he knew that when Peter turned back, he would be in a position to effectively strengthen his brothers. God handpicked you, knowing full well every mistake you would ever make. He's not asking you to live a perfect life. He's asking you to turn and strengthen your brothers. He wants to turn your mess into a message.

DONNA PARTOW
This Isn't the Life I Signed Up For

Weeds

See to it that no one falls short of the grace of God and that no bitter root grows up to cause trouble and defile many.

Hebrews 12:15 niv

I'm no gardener, but even I know that weeds are no good for a garden. So when the flower bed in front of our house got about knee high, I decided it was time I had to do something.

My task seemed to be going well until I turned and looked back at my progress. While I had removed most of the weeds, there were dozens of little tiny sprouts left just poking through the soil. My husband saw my plight and helped me out.

When I came out to check on him, I found he had taken the hose and soaked the soil before he began. Two weeks later the evidence was clear; my area was once again full of weeds, while his was blooming with flowers.

I've found forgiveness to be a lot like that flower bed. When we try to pull out the weeds of pain inflicted on us by others, we often leave the root of the problem deep within the soil. Left undealt with, those wounds will begin to fester and grow as surely as those roots left in the soil grew back to crowd out the flowers. But if we soak our lives with the Word of God, it softens the soil for God to remove those things which have wounded us and are choking out the blossoms of His grace and mercy that He so wants to see bloom in our lives.

MISSY HORSFALL
CIRCLE OF FRIENDS

Happiness = Health

May my friends sing and shout for joy.
May they always say, "Praise the greatness of the LORD,
who loves to see his servants do well."

PSALM 35:27 NCV

Good relationships are crucial to our success in life. We can't live well without them. Studies have been done on the importance of positive social support systems with regard to our health. The conclusions have been that good relationships contribute to better health and a lower death rate. That is one good reason why we should pray for each one of our relationships to be uplifting, edifying, encouraging, and always glorifying to God.

We know when we are in a good relationship. And we know when we have a relationship that is troubling. . . . While good relationships enhance our lives, bad ones are far more damaging than we think. We must do what we can to protect and nurture the good ones but stop tolerating the bad ones. . . . I'm not saying you have to get rid of every relationship that goes through a difficult time. What I am saying is that when a relationship becomes destructive to you, put a stop to it. Don't permit it to carry on like that. It is not of God, and it doesn't glorify Him. . . . If someone continually causes you to feel bad about yourself, your family, or your life, release that person to God and pray for [him or her] from afar.

STORMIE OMARTIAN
The Power of a Praying Life

Learning to Love

Follow God's example, therefore, as dearly loved children and walk in the way of love, just as Christ loved us and gave himself up for us as a fragrant offering and sacrifice to God.

EPHESIANS 5:1–2 NIV

I wish it weren't so, but learning to love others, especially difficult people, has been the biggest challenge in my Christian life. Whether it was an ornery child, a mother with Alzheimer's, or a young unbelieving husband, I've failed countless times in what mattered most—loving them as God does. I've worn out my knees begging God's forgiveness for irritability, critical words, even wanting to walk away at times. You'd think I'd have learned sooner that duplicating God's love is impossible. It's the one thing we can't fake for long and Satan can't imitate. I've finally figured out why.

Only Jesus can do it. How simple! We love like Jesus only when His poured-in love spills out. His love has nothing at all to do with feelings. It's not gushy, sentimental, or showy, which gives me some relief. It has everything to do with giving, but nothing to do with money; rich and poor alike receive their supply "free" at the same bank. The key is having a heart willing to obey His word and do His will, no matter what. That's the rub.

Need more love for others today? Just ask with a surrendered heart. And watch out. God's love is a magnet in a fallen world, drawing others to Christ when we don't even know it.

VIRELLE KIDDER
THE BEST LIFE AIN'T EASY, BUT IT'S WORTH IT

Are You Willing?

One who was there had been an invalid for thirty-eight years. When Jesus saw him lying there and learned that he had been in this condition for a long time, he asked him, "Do you want to get well?"

JOHN 5:5–6 NIV

Jesus once asked a man, "Do you want to get well?" The man in question had been sick for a long time. He was identified by it; people recognized him as the one who could do nothing to help himself. Jesus' question required a lot of him. Healing in this case happened in a moment, but he would have to live out the rest of his life making different choices. When he lay by the pool, those who passed him might have thrown some coins toward his plight or a kind word, a moment of sympathy and human connection. If he was healed, he must become part of the healing of others.

Being healed by Christ teaches you one thing for sure: We are healed to come to others in Jesus' name, offering the same healing. We are no longer at liberty to be part of the problem; we are given the joy of being part of the solution. Do you want to get well? Those who have been broken and restored by Christ have a God-given ability to connect with others in pain and offer hope and healing.

When Christ heals us, when we get up and walk again, we discover there is work to be done. We have begun to live again!

SHEILA WALSH
THE HEARTACHE NO ONE SEES

Practicing Forgiveness

"And forgive us our sins, as we forgive
those who sin against us.
And don't let us yield to temptation."

LUKE 11:4 NLT

Forgiveness is not forgetting the pain, nor is it approving of the wrong actions of others. Forgiveness does not erase the memory of what has happened, nor does forgiveness mean everything will turn out okay. There are still many times when I identify with the psalmist: "I've cried my eyes out; I feel hollow inside. My life leaks away, groan by groan; my years fade out in sighs. My troubles have worn me out, turned my bones to powder" (Psalm 31:10 MSG). But I continue to learn that forgiving is a choice that brings healing—probably more to the giver than to the recipient. When we forgive, we do not change the circumstances or injustices of the past. What we change is the future—for ourselves and for the ones we have forgiven. It is the most freeing choice we can make.

Some days Gene and I blame ourselves for not being better parents. On other days, we seek forgiveness for all of our self-condemnation. On some days we blame God, and on other days we thank Him for His mercies, which are new every day we continue to walk this bumpy road (Lamentations 3:22–23). We're simply trying to be real about blame and forgiveness. And it's very complicated. We have each other and that's good.

CAROL KENT
A New Kind of Normal

Give Thanks for Personal Talents

*Though I speak with the tongues of men and
of angels, and have not charity, I am become as
sounding brass, or a tinkling cymbal.*

1 CORINTHIANS 13:1 KJV

You may be the most talented person in your company
at your job description, but if you aren't gracious, too, you
may just seem like noise to the people around you. Who
can stand someone who toots his own horn (or clangs her
own cymbal) so much that others can't wait to get away
from the sound?

Obnoxiousness isn't part of a Christian's job
description. The hallmarks of faith are graciousness and
love (or charity, as this version calls it). So when you do
well in your work, thank God for the gifts He's given
you that allow you to serve Him well. Be thankful that

He's given folks who helped you learn your job and who continue to make your work possible. And appreciate the particular gifts of others who work with you.

No matter how gifted you are spiritually or skills-wise, no one appreciates someone who's so full of himself that there's no room for God or anyone else. So have some charity on your job, and you won't just be noise—you'll shed the light of Jesus' love.

PAMELA L. MCQUADE
DAILY WISDOM FOR THE WORKPLACE

Overflowing Love

He shall be a vessel unto honour, sanctified, and meet for the master's use, and prepared unto every good work.

2 TIMOTHY 2:21 KJV

The love of Christ is not an absorbing, but a radiating love. The more we love Him, the more we shall most certainly love others. Some have not much natural power of loving, but the love of Christ will strengthen it. Some have had the springs of love dried up by some terrible earthquake. They will find "fresh springs" in Jesus, and the gentle flow will be purer and deeper than the old torrent could ever be. Some have been satisfied that it should rush in a narrow channel, but He will cause it to overflow into many another, and widen its course of blessing.

There is no love so deep and wide as that which is kept for Jesus. It flows both fuller and farther when it flows only through Him. Then, too, it will be a power for Him. It will always be unconsciously working for Him. In drawing others to ourselves by it, we shall be necessarily drawing them nearer to the fountain of our love, never drawing them away from it. It is the great magnet of His love which alone can draw any heart to Him; but when our own are thoroughly yielded to its mighty influence, they will be so magnetized that He will condescend to use them in this way.

Frances Ridley Havergal
Kept for the Master's Use

"Shun Flattery"

Faithful are the wounds of a friend;
but the kisses of an enemy are deceitful.

PROVERBS 27:6 KJV

Before 1840, my friends had nearly spoiled me with their praises. At least I began to feel my own importance as a poet a little too much; and so the superintendent, Mr. Jones, thought something ought to be done to curb such rising vanity. One morning after breakfast I was summoned to the office. It was an impressive occasion, and I remember what Mr. Jones said almost word for word:

"Fanny, I am sorry you have allowed yourself to be carried away by what others have said about your verses. True, you have written a number of poems of real merit; but how far do they fall short of the standard that you might attain. Shun a flatterer, Fanny, as you would a viper; for no true friend would deceive you with words of flattery. Remember that whatever talent you possess belongs wholly to God; and that you ought to give Him the credit for all that you do."

In years afterward I gradually came to realize that his advice was worth more than the price of rubies; and if I am justified in drawing any analogy from my own experience, I would say that a little kindly advice is better than a great deal of scolding. For a single word, if spoken in a friendly spirit, may be sufficient to turn one from a dangerous error.

FANNY CROSBY
MEMORIES OF EIGHTY YEARS

Love and Friendship

Charity suffereth long, and is kind; charity envieth not;
charity vaunteth not itself, is not puffed up.

1 Corinthians 13:4 KJV

Friendship is a wonderful thing. The love of friendship is often stronger than the love of brotherhood and sisterhood. There is a cord of tenderness and appreciation binding those who are friends which is lovely beyond words to express it. Every truehearted girl loves her friends with a devotion that beautifies her life and enlarges her heart. She who is unable to be true in friendship has little of value in her.

A friendship does not grow up spontaneously. It must have a good soil in which to take root, good seed from which to start, and care and cultivation, in order to become its best. The good soil is sincerity and truth coupled with kindness and affection. The good seed is love and appreciation. And it must be watched closely that no weeds of jealousy or envy creep in, and the soil must be constantly stirred by kind acts, words of appreciation and affection, and mutual admiration. There dare be no selfish interests nor evil suspicions in true friendship. The smallest bit of mistrust will blight it like frost. Friendship is tender, but it is beautiful.

MABEL HALE
BEAUTIFUL GIRLHOOD

God of All Comfort

Blessed be the God and Father of our Lord Jesus Christ,
the Father of mercies and God of all comfort,
who comforts us in all our tribulation.

2 CORINTHIANS 1:3–4 NKJV

Such Christians, although they profess to be the followers of the God of all comfort, spread gloom and discomfort around them wherever they go; and it is out of the question for them to hope that they can induce anyone else to believe that this beautiful name, by which He has announced Himself, is anything more than a pious phrase, which in reality means nothing at all. And the manifestly uncomfortable religious lives of so many Christians are, I am very much afraid, responsible for a large part of the unbelief of the world.

The apostle says that we are to be living epistles known and read of all men; and the question as to what men read in us is of far more vital importance to the spread of Christ's kingdom than we half the time realize. It is not what we say that tells, but what we are.

It is easy enough to say a great many beautiful things about God being the God of all comfort; but unless we know what it is to be really and truly comforted ourselves, we might as well talk to the winds. People must read in our lives what they hear in our words, or all our preaching is worse than useless. It would be well for us to ask ourselves what they are reading in us. Is it comfort or discomfort that voices itself in our daily walk and life?

HANNAH WHITALL SMITH
THE GOD OF ALL COMFORT

A Hospitable Heart

*After [Lydia] was baptized, along with everyone in her
household, she said in a surge of hospitality,
"If you're confident that I'm in this with you and believe in
the Master truly, come home with me and be my guests."
We hesitated, but she wouldn't take no for an answer.*

ACTS 16:15 MSG

Lydia, a dealer in purple cloth, worked hard at her trade.
The Bible does not tell us much else about her except that
she was a worshipper of God.

One day during their travels, Paul and his companions
stopped to pray by the river outside the city gate of
Philippi. They met a group of women there that included
Lydia. She listened to Paul's message and accepted Jesus.
After Lydia was baptized, she insisted the men come home
with her and be her guests. As was customary for a hostess,

she likely prepared and served them food and gave them a place to rest and pray. She showed hospitality in the name of the Lord.

You can follow Lydia's lead. Whether your home is small or large, you can choose to be hospitable. Invite a friend who needs a pick-me-up to join you for a meal during the week. Ask a single mom and her children to come over for a pizza and movie night. If elderly neighbors are unable to get out, take your hospitality to them! Bake them some cookies or take them flowers from your garden.

EMILY BIGGERS
DAILY ENCOURAGEMENT FOR SINGLE WOMEN

I Have Planned Ahead for You

Nevertheless I am continually with You; You have taken hold of my right hand. With Your counsel You will guide me.

Psalm 73:23–24 NASB

Behold, am I a God that is afar off, and not a God that is near? For in the midst of difficulties, I will be your support. In the darkness, I am your Light; there is no darkness that can hide My face from the eye of faith. My beauty and My radiance are all the lovelier in darkness.

In grief, My comfort is more poignant. In failure, My encouragement the most welcome. In loneliness, the touch of My presence more tender. You are hidden in Me, and I will multiply both the wisdom and the strength in due proportion to meet the demands of every occasion.

I am the Lord your God. I know no limitations. I know no lack. I need not reserve My stores, for I always have a fresh supply. You can by no means ever exhaust My infinite resources. Let your heart run wild. Let your imagination go vagabond. No extravagance of human thought can ever plumb the depths of My planning and provision for My children.

Rejoice, therefore, and face each day with joy; for I have planned ahead for you, and made all necessary arrangements and reservations. I am your guide and benefactor. Put your hand in Mine.

FRANCES J. ROBERTS
Come Away My Beloved

Gentle Care

When you sin against [your brother or sister] in this way and wound their weak conscience, you sin against Christ.

1 Corinthians 8:12 NIV

The young Christians of Corinth were probably a power-packed bunch when it came to witnessing. They keenly felt their past sins and appreciated the forgiveness they'd found in Christ. But they were also still so close to their unforgiven days that they did all they could to avoid every temptation. So they insisted that no faithful Christian should eat meat offered to the idols they'd recently worshipped. It obviously created quite a furor in the congregation, since Paul had to address the subject.

Paul explained some of this to the Corinthians who'd known Jesus longer and asked them to treat the new Christians gently by not condemning something they meant for good, even if it was inconvenient. He asked them not to harm a brother by pushing him to do something his conscience said was wrong. To do so was to also hurt Christ.

Real Christians can differ on many minor issues of doctrine or practice. Those small things can become like sand in the wheels of faith, disrupting the church on many levels. Or they can become opportunities to show the love we share. Which will they be for you today?

PAMELA L. MCQUADE
DAILY WISDOM FOR THE WORKPLACE

Putting Out the
Welcome Mat

*Do not forget to entertain strangers,
for by so doing some have unwittingly entertained angels.*

HEBREWS 13:2 NKJV

When I was a child growing up in a large family and a small home, we always had company. . . . Most summer evenings, ten, twenty, or more neighbors and relatives ended up at our house on the front porch. When they did, there was talking, laughing, storytelling (*mostly* storytelling), and joy. Immoderate joy, really, that welcomed everyone to come in and make themselves at home. And it happened all the time. Even when the Avon lady came, she stayed all day. . . .

Having spent all of my adult life in ministry, that hospitality trend has continued. Because of my parents, it's always seemed natural to bring people home with me.

I've brought them home when they needed someplace to stay, or when they were sick, or hurting, or hungry, or for no other reason than that I enjoyed the pleasure of their company. . . .

Hospitality is underrated! It's not just an old-fashioned idea that people used to have time to enjoy because life was duller and less complicated. Hospitality is God's idea. It's a joyful, welcoming idea.

First Peter 4:9 says, "Be hospitable to one another without grumbling" (NKJV). That's in the context of the verse before that, which says to love one another fervently, and the following verse, which says to minister to each other. Practicing hospitality is important to God and us. . . . It is kingdom work. Be welcoming. There is no greater joy.

MARY GRAHAM
CONTAGIOUS JOY

Love God, Love People

He answered: " 'Love the Lord your God with all your heart and with all your soul and with all your strength and with all your mind'; and, 'Love your neighbor as yourself.' "

LUKE 10:27 NIV

Many Christians think that following God involves adhering to a set of rules and regulations. I remember one Christian author posing the question (in fact, I think it was a chapter title in one of his books), "Can a Christian drive a BMW?" I'm pretty sure his answer was "No." The Pharisees had more rules than you could shake a stick at! And they followed the letter of the law with tremendous determination and religious zeal.

Was Jesus pleased with them? No. He told them, in essence, "You're making this way more complicated than it needs to be." I like the way Augustine put it: "Love

God and do whatever you want." If you love God, you'll walk in close communion with Him. If you walk in close communion with Him, you'll become more and more like Him. Since God loves people, you'll love people, too. If you love people, you'll be a loving person who does the right thing from the heart rather than from a rule book. Love God. Love people. Don't worry about the rest.

DONNA PARTOW
BECOMING THE WOMAN I WANT TO BE

Spread the Joy!

Love is kind.

1 CORINTHIANS 13:4 NIV

*E*very single day we encounter joy stealers. You know the type—rude cashiers, angry drivers, inconsiderate coworkers, and even grouchy family members. You'll have an opportunity (probably before breakfast) to get mad, but you can choose kindness instead.

Not long ago I encountered one of those joy stealers at the supermarket. This cashier was angry. Whatever the cause, this gal was not in a good mood. As she scanned my items, she was muttering under her breath. Though I hated to disturb her, I had a few coupons to use, which I slid toward her.

Glaring at me, she snapped, "You're supposed to hand those to me at the beginning of the transaction."

Ever been there?

Now, what I wanted to say was, "Listen, sister, I'll report your rudeness to your supervisor. Don't push me." Instead, I answered, "Oh, I'm sorry. I wasn't aware of that policy. If it's too much trouble, I can just save them and use them the next time I go grocery shopping."

She didn't even respond, so I continued.

"I bet you get tired of rule breakers like me, eh?"

She cracked a smile.

Before she scanned my last can of green beans, we were best buddies. She not only let me use my coupons, but she gave me a couple of extra ones she had at her station. I didn't let this cashier steal my joy. Instead, I gave her some of mine. You can do the same. Joy is contagious.

Be a carrier and spread it everywhere you go.

MICHELLE MEDLOCK ADAMS
Secrets of Happiness

Team Player

I planted the seed, Apollos watered it,
but God has been making it grow.

1 Corinthians 3:6 NIV

$\mathcal{D}$id you know you are part of a team—with God? It's true! You're part of a squad to bring His good news to a hurting world.

Paul was part of a team, too. He came to Corinth and preached the gospel. A man named Apollos helped these new Christians grow. But it wasn't long before Corinthian Christians started dividing up according to which leader they thought was best. Some boasted of their connection with Paul, while others claimed that being ministered to by Apollos was better. Paul pointed out that God caused spiritual growth, no matter who did the preaching.

Whether it's in church or the workplace, recognize the importance of what Paul is saying here. No one gets results alone—everything's a team effort, no matter what your chore is. So recognize the input others have. Treat your coworkers as a team and help that team to work at its peak efficiency.

You may have had an idea, but others created it, advertised it, and took it out to the marketplace. Then people bought it. In the business world, that's growth. None of it would have happened if God hadn't worked through you.

So recognize your place in the team and give thanks for those who help you—God especially!

PAMELA L. McQUADE
DAILY WISDOM FOR THE WORKPLACE

Best Friends

Do not be misled: "Bad company corrupts good character."

1 Corinthians 15:33 niv

So much is made of the importance of the right kind of friends in the Bible that we can't treat this part of our lives lightly. "The righteous should choose his friends carefully, for the way of the wicked leads them astray" (Proverbs 12:26 nkjv). If it's true that we become like the friends we spend time with, then we must select our friends wisely. The main quality to look for in a close friend is not how attractive, talented, wealthy, smart, influential, clever, or popular they are. It's how much they love and fear God. The person who will do what it takes to live in the perfect will of God is the kind of friend who imparts something of the goodness of the Lord to you every time you are with them.

God doesn't want us to be unequally yoked with

unbelievers, but that doesn't mean we should have nothing to do with anyone who doesn't know the Lord. Far from it. We are God's tool to reach others for His kingdom. But our closest relationships, the ones that influence us the most, need to be with people who love and fear God. If you don't have close friends who are believers, pray for godly and desirable friends to come into your life.

STORMIE OMARTIAN
THE POWER OF A PRAYING WOMAN

I Love You . . .
Even in the Hard Times

A friend loves at all times.

PROVERBS 17:17 NKJV

A woman walked her best friend through a difficult season. Health problems, a death in the family, and a serious bout with depression threatened to be her friend's undoing. Still, the woman stuck with it. Even when her friend insisted she didn't want anyone around. *Especially* when her friend insisted she didn't want anyone around.

Have you ever walked a friend through a tough season? Been there when she faced depression or pain? Held her hand as she mourned the loss of someone she loved? Walked with her through an illness or job-related challenge? Cried with her as her marriage came to a painful end? If so, then you truly know what it means to love at all times. Friendship—true friendship—runs deeper than the unexpected challenges of life.

Today, think of a friend who is going through a particularly difficult season. What can you do to lift her spirits? How can you encourage her to keep going? Should you send a card? Flowers? Make a phone call? Write an encouraging note? Take her to see a movie? Remember: God-breathed love pours itself out at all times.

JANICE HANNA
DAILY ENCOURAGEMENT FOR SINGLE WOMEN

Love, Friendship, and Faith

"My command is this: Love each other as I have loved you.
Greater love has no one than this:
to lay down one's life for one's friends.
You are my friends if you do what I command."

JOHN 15:12–14 NIV

Miss Andy lived in the dormitory with us girls. Daily we saw lived out the high principle of Jesus' words in Matthew 25:40 (NIV), "Truly I tell you, whatever you did for one of the least of these brothers and sisters of mine, you did for me." She, like the other teachers, showed us the meaning of sacrifice. She laid down her life for us. Love always means sacrifice.

Miss Andy was a woman with a gentle and quiet spirit, a radiant smile, total selflessness. She not only taught school. She planned the menus, did the shopping and countless other errands. When the school lost its only two paid employees, the cooks, it was Miss Andy who took over the task—not neglecting her teaching responsibilities. How was it possible? God knows. . . .

Jane [Miss Andy] was—will always be—to me an icon of lovingkindness and quiet, hidden selflessness. On the last day of her life she taught school as she had done for fifty-nine years, and then cooked dinner. Like the woman who poured perfume on Jesus' head, she did what she could.

ELISABETH ELLIOT
SECURE IN THE EVERLASTING ARMS

Difficult People

Do not turn your freedom into an opportunity for the flesh,
but through love serve one another.

GALATIANS 5:13 NASB

In the classic movie *An Affair to Remember*, Deborah Kerr asks Cary Grant, "What makes life so difficult?" to which he responds, "People?"

Yes, people tend to make our lives difficult. But they also make life worth living. The trick is not to let the biting words or nefarious deeds of others become glaring giants that make us flee or weigh us down with hate and resentment.

The only way David stood up to the giant Goliath was by turning his problem over to the Lord and relying on His strength and power. Then, acting in faith, David prevailed with the weapons at hand—a slingshot and one smooth stone.

Sometimes, like David, we need to turn our skirmishes with others over to the Lord. Then, by using our weapons—God's Word and a steadfast faith—we need to love and forgive others as God loves and forgives us.

Always keep in mind that, although we may not like to admit it, we have all said and done some pretty awful things ourselves, making the lives of others difficult. Yet God has forgiven us *and* continues to love us.

So do the right thing. Pull your feet out of the mire of unforgiveness, sidestep verbal retaliation, and stand tall in the freedom of love and forgiveness.

DONNA K. MALTESE
WHISPERS OF WISDOM FOR BUSY WOMEN

Loneliness and Happiness
Don't Mix

God has said, "Never will I leave you;
never will I forsake you."

HEBREWS 13:5 NIV

Mother Teresa once said, "The most terrible poverty is loneliness and the feeling of being unloved."

If you're feeling lonely today, happiness may seem far off. Loneliness has a way of consuming your life, leaving little room for anything else—especially happiness. You may be alone due to circumstances beyond your control. Maybe a recent move left all your friends behind. Or maybe you're in a great marriage and surrounded by friends—yet you still feel lonely.

It happens.

Whatever your situation, God understands and cares. He wants you to know that you are never alone—no matter how lonely you might feel at this moment. He promises in His Word never to leave you nor forsake you. That's great to know, isn't it? God is right there with you, loving you through your good and bad times.

God wants you to escape the loneliness you're feeling and embrace the joy He has to offer. Sure, that's easier said than done, but you can take a step away from loneliness and toward happiness right now. Here's how: Get your focus off yourself and meet someone else's needs today. The devil wants to keep you in your own isolated little world. But don't let him. Leave your comfort zone and reach out and touch someone with the love of Jesus today. The sooner you start helping others, the sooner your loneliness will be replaced with purpose and joy.

MICHELLE MEDLOCK ADAMS
SECRETS OF HAPPINESS

Give Prayer

Give generously to the poor, not grudgingly,
for the LORD your God will bless you in everything you do.

DEUTERONOMY 15:10 NLT

Our happiness is related to our own generosity. "He who has a generous eye will be blessed, for he gives of his bread to the poor" (Proverbs 22:9 NKJV). People who have a generous eye look out for others in need. They watch to see who they can help and how they can do it. And in the process, God rewards them. . . .

There are many ways to meet the needs of others if you just ask God to show you. Give to other people without expecting anything back from them. Keep the focus on giving to please God. I have found that when I need breakthrough or release in my life, I check to see if there are ways I should be giving to others. Perhaps I have something they need or there is something I can do or say that would help them or be an encouragement. Don't ever feel you have nothing to give, because that is never true. You have the Lord, who is the source of your supply. One of the greatest gifts someone ever gave me was a promise to pray for me. That was more valuable to me than anything. I have also given that same gift to others. And I have found that even those who don't know the Lord are still surprisingly happy to receive prayer.

STORMIE OMARTIAN
THE POWER OF A PRAYING LIFE

Lend a Hand to Others

Let no debt remain outstanding,
except the continuing debt to love one another,
for whoever loves others has fulfilled the law.

ROMANS 13:8 NIV

On your first job or a new one, someone probably helped you get a start or learn the ropes at a new company. As your career has gone on, people have assisted you in other ways— the new staff person has given you a hand when you were overloaded with work and never complained about the extra hours, or your boss has taken up some slack for you.

Whether or not you feel like admitting it, you are in their debt. But they've already been paid by the company, so what could you do about it? Lots. You may not pay back your boss today, but someday he'll need help. Maybe you can help train a new employee. Your new coworker may need help on how to handle a situation. Or maybe you can offer to double-check something for her.

When you can't repay a debt, you can show your love for the other person by lending a hand. And if you can't give that help to the person who helped you, pass it on to another coworker. If everyone does that, your company will be a great place to work in.

PAMELA L. McQUADE
DAILY WISDOM FOR THE WORKPLACE

The Blessing of Encouragement

In his grace, God has given us different gifts
for doing certain things well. . . .
If your gift is to encourage others, be encouraging.

ROMANS 12:6, 8 NLT

What happiness it brings *me* to share a glad word
with. . .hurting hearts and help bring restoration with an
infusion of God's hope! When something is restored it
pops back in place, like an out-of-joint bone that is popped
back into alignment, relieving the pain. Encouragement
works like an emotional chiropractor—and both "doctor"
and patient benefit from the treatment. As someone said,
"Encouragement is a double blessing. Both giver and
receiver are blessed."

It's easy to be an encourager. We can encourage
someone with a cheery phone call, a quick visit—or just

a smile. One of my favorite ways to encourage others is by writing a quick note. Usually I jot something down on a silly cartoon I've seen somewhere. The message doesn't have to be long. Brief and sincere notes can uplift the receiver as much as a bouquet of flowers—perhaps more. If you find it hard to express yourself, begin by telling your friend about some kindness she has done for you. Remind her how much her friendship means to you, then offer your own encouragement to her.

BARBARA JOHNSON
LIVING SOMEWHERE BETWEEN ESTROGEN AND DEATH

Favors

May the LORD show you his
kindness and have mercy on you.

NUMBERS 6:25 NCV

When you surprise someone with a gracious kindness,
you experience the blessing of being favored yourself. . . .

But what, exactly, is *favor*? As I studied this word,
it intrigued me. Webster's dictionary says it is "friendly
regard shown toward another, especially by a superior."
It's "approving consideration or attention" or an "effort
in one's behalf or interest." To me, the most surprising
revelation about this unique word was that it can be "a
special privilege or right granted or conceded." This is the
kind of favor bestowed by God. He doesn't ask us to earn
extra points on "the goodness chart." He doesn't hand out
merit badges. Rather, his favor is *granted*; it's a surprise

blessing. It's undeserved and free! To be shown favor is to experience the smile of God through someone who graces our life with resources, approval, encouragement, opportunity, or hope when we have come upon an obstacle too overwhelming to deal with on our own. . . .

[Today,] humbly receive God's favor through the kind hands of people who genuinely care.

Carol Kent
Between a Rock and a Grace Place

Powerful Prayers

The mind governed by the Spirit is life and peace.

ROMANS 8:6 NIV

I once traveled by car through the mountains of California from Los Angeles to San Francisco. It is one of my weak points that I am afraid of driving through mountains with Americans. They usually drive at such great speed. Along one side of the road was a deep chasm, and, moreover, there were many dangerous curves. I knew from experience what to do when the demon of fear entered my heart. He had called on me many a time during my imprisonment in Germany, and I would then begin to sing. Singing always helps. Try it yourself sometime; fear and anxiety will vanish when you sing.

So I sang one hymn after another, until my host, the driver, said teasingly, "Are you afraid?"

"Yes," I said, "that is why I am singing."

But this time it was all to no avail. Every time we approached a curve, I would think, *If another car is coming towards us from beyond that curve, we shall certainly crash into each other!* And, thoroughly frightened, I would stop singing.

No, singing did not help me now. Then I tried to dispel my fear by prayer, and I prayed. . . . I prayed for everyone who came into my thoughts, people with whom I had travelled, those who had been in prison with me, my school friends of years ago. I do not know how long I continued in prayer, but this I do know, my fear was gone. Interceding for others had released myself.

CORRIE TEN BOOM
AMAZING LOVE

Sisters in Christ

Friends love through all kinds of weather.

PROVERBS 17:17 MSG

Throughout my life, God has blessed me with some relationships that have transcended friendship to reveal a bond of sisterhood in Christ. Theresa belongs in that category.

During my quiet time with the Lord one evening, I came across the stories in 1 Samuel that chronicle the friendship between David and Jonathan. . . . It occurred to me that as King Saul's son, Jonathan *should* have been the next king of Israel. But even when David was anointed king and was promised everything that was rightfully Jonathan's, Jonathan still risked his life for David. It was such a vivid portrayal of friendship. I wondered if I could be that selfless for a friend.

When I told Theresa that I was expecting my first

baby, she was ecstatic! . . . What made her joy that much more precious was that Theresa had been trying to have a child for over a year with no success. . . . As she jumped up and down, shrieking with glee for me, I realized that Theresa was just like Jonathan. Even when I was granted everything that she had ever desired, Theresa willingly laid aside her own sorrow to share in my happiness. . . .

A few weeks later, Michael and I lost our precious baby, and it was Theresa who came to sit with me while I was overcome with grief. . . . She made me laugh when my heart was broken. But more important, she loved me with the love of a sister in Christ.

ALLISON SHAW
KISSES OF SUNSHINE FOR WOMEN

"Don't Hate Me Because I'm Beautiful"

Yet you are stupid enough to brag,
and it is wrong to be so proud.

JAMES 4:16 CEV

You've seen the commercial. The gorgeous girl whips her long, luscious locks to the side; then with her pouty, very glossy lips, she utters, "Don't hate me because I'm beautiful."

But in reality, we would hate her—not because she's beautiful. No, we'd hate her because she loves to brag on herself. Nobody likes a bragger. We all know someone like that girl in the commercial. She might not be as blatant, but you can bet your lipstick she'll find a way to sneak in a boast or two.

She might not even brag about herself. She might brag about her new home. Or worse, she might drone on and on about her super-accomplished kids. No matter what she brags about, it's enough to make you want to run for the hills.

Are you a bragger? It's an easy habit to fall into, but it's also a very dangerous one. The Bible says that pride comes before a fall, and that fall may plop you right into a pit of loneliness. People will hate you—but it won't be because you're beautiful.

If you're struggling with the bad habit of bragging, ask God to put a watch over your mouth. Make a conscious decision to listen more than you talk. Learn to trust God to raise you up. You'll discover that you won't have to brag on yourself to feel important. You'll win friends and influence people, and they'll love you because you're beautiful on the inside. After all, that's where it really counts!

MICHELLE MEDLOCK ADAMS
SECRETS OF BEAUTY

Together

Together you are the body of Christ,
and each one of you is a part of that body.

1 CORINTHIANS 12:27 NCV

$\mathcal{D}$o you ever struggle with jealousy? That awful, twisted feeling of wanting what someone else has—"Oh, I wish I could go on a vacation like that. . ."; "If only I got paid that salary. . ."; or "If I had money/a job/an opportunity like that and if my children/home/car/life were different. . ." We look at others' lives and ours and come away dissatisfied.

Not a good place to be—Proverbs 14:30 (NKJV) says envy is "rottenness to the bones," and James tells us that "where envy and self-seeking exist, confusion *and every evil thing* are there" (James 3:16 NKJV). Peter tells us to rid ourselves of "all malice and all deceit, hypocrisy, envy, and slander of every kind" (1 Peter 2:1 NKJV). Have you noticed how jealousy and envy are closely associated with more bad attitudes and sin? One thing just leads to another. To go from jealousy and envy to malice is to actually desire someone else's pain!

Now that I've recognized it, how do I get rid of it? Peter goes on in verses 2 and 3 (NIV): "Like newborn babies, crave pure spiritual milk, so that by it you may grow up in your salvation, now that you have tasted that the Lord is good." God's Word is the only thing that can set my attitude straight!

The secret is found in 1 Corinthians 12:24–27. When one of us suffers, we all suffer; when one of us is honored, we share that honor. We are *together* the body of Christ.

MISSY HORSFALL
CIRCLE OF FRIENDS

Necessary Blessing

*Real wisdom, God's wisdom, begins with a holy life
and is characterized by getting along with others.*

JAMES 3:17 MSG

I know how hard it is to be friends with women. Believe
me, it takes a lot of work. Men are so much easier to be
with. They aren't so emotional. They're fun to be with. But
that's no excuse to avoid women altogether. And if you
haven't already experienced it, one day you will find that
you really need women friends. I believe that God made
us for communion with other women. He didn't make us
so that all our lives we would be surrounded by men only.
That brings a whole mess of problems when it comes time
to pair off. Jealousy, the risk of affairs, all of that enters
when you mainly have friends of the opposite sex. And the
truth is that certain things you can only get from other
women, and certain things we should only *give* to other
women. . . .

Girls are important. And as you get older, what you are doing when you surround yourself with women (and by that I mean you have at least three good girlfriends) is preparing yourself for the future. Men can come and go, but if you keep your friendships strong, you will always have a shoulder to cry on.

HAYLEY DiMARCO
MEAN GIRLS ALL GROWN UP

In This Together

You can develop a healthy, robust community that lives right with God and enjoy its results only if you do the hard work of getting along with each other.

JAMES 3:17 MSG

I thank God He knew we would gain comfort and joy in relating. . .usually. So He gave us each other. Have you noticed the recent surge of interest in celebrating friendship? Tons of cards, books, and clubs are devoted to friendship. And I've watched thousands of women over the years attend Women of Faith conferences dressed alike. Sometimes a hundred women will wear matching T-shirts or tiaras. I love that. It breeds a spirit of camaraderie.

Girlfriends are so connected. We "get" each other. You know, the monthly cycle stuff, the flashes, and the moods from down under (and I don't mean Australia). I think we girls feel less alone in our feminine experiences when we can gab about them with someone who's having the same chaos in her anatomy. Guys just glaze over when we whine about cramps, water gain, or our hurt feelings, whereas women commiserate.

Commiserating is rooted in community. And community gives us a sense of people coming together for a common purpose. Now, that sounds friendly. . .unless you watch *Survivor* or *The Amazing Race*. I've noticed even members on the same team get on each other's nerves; yet let one of them be isolated or separated from "his people," and all he can think about is reuniting with the very ones who had frayed him. Aren't we a strange lot?

PATSY CLAIRMONT
DANCING BONES

Read Scripture

*Now the Berean Jews. . .received the message
with great eagerness and examined the Scriptures
every day to see if what Paul said was true.*

ACTS 17:11 NIV

You hear a lot of "spiritual" talk in church, on your favorite Christian radio station, and from friends. How much of it agrees? Spiritual discussions, at work or church, may get intense. Two friends may each think they have the method for really worshipping God. Both seem so sincere, yet they tell you different things. You want to believe correctly. When you've heard a couple of different "truths," how do you know which is right?

Don't be afraid to check the scriptures people quote or to compare ideas against God's Word. After all, Paul applauded the Bereans for doing that when he came into town with his gospel teaching. Christianity isn't a mindless faith. And when you read those scriptures, read more than that one verse, and you may discover the truth. The paragraph or page around it can change the entire meaning of a sentence.

But don't stop with reading a few scriptures only when you need an answer. Read your Bible every day. Then when an issue comes up, verses from other parts of the Bible can come to your mind, and God can constantly show you *His* truth.

Lord, spiritual talk sure can be confusing, and I don't want to be distracted from Your truth. Help me search and find it in Your Word.

PAMELA L. MCQUADE
DAILY WISDOM FOR THE WORKPLACE

The Moustache-Waxing
Moments of Life

*God will yet fill your mouth with laughter
and your lips with shouts of joy.*

JOB 8:21 NCV

The salon I frequent is a large one, and on this particular day every chair was taken. . . . As I sat with someone working on my nails and another on my feet, a new employee approached me and asked if I would like to have my eyebrows waxed. I politely declined because the last time I had that procedure done, it removed most of my forehead as well. With all the determination of a terrier, this girl was not going to be left with idle hands and continued in a loud voice, "How about your moustache? Can I wax your moustache?"

"Moustache?" I said. "Moustache!"

That evening I asked [my son] at dinner if he was aware that his mother had a moustache.

"Of course not, Mom," he said, laughing.

I was relieved but only for a moment.

"You don't have a moustache, but you do have a big hair growing out of the side of your face," he said. "Actually, you're quite a hairy person. . . ."

As I sat in the bath later that night reviewing my role as the missing link, something else occurred to me—I couldn't wait to tell [my friends] so that we could all enjoy a good laugh together. That's one of the great joys of friendship. We get to share our triumphs and tragedies, the unexpected joys, and the petty indignities of life. As I slathered on a little more lotion than normal that night, I thought of Solomon's words: "Just as lotions and fragrance give sensual delight, a sweet friendship refreshes the soul" (Proverbs 27:9 MSG).

SHEILA WALSH
CONTAGIOUS JOY

Service with a Smile

Serve wholeheartedly, as if you were
serving the Lord, not people.

EPHESIANS 6:7 NIV

Sometimes others will get the wrong impression as we humble ourselves to serve them. Don't worry about it. Let them! It's not about them. It's not about you. But it *is* all about God. Those who are important to Him must be important to us if we're truly in love with the Lover of Our Souls. We will want to serve His family. We will want to serve those He longs to make a part of the family, no matter how unlovable they might be. He loves them and that should be enough for us.

So how do we accomplish getting past ourselves, past the bad attitudes of others, and into His heart? Through the giving of our gifts and talents, a loving attitude, a humble disposition, and our acts of service. (To me, that is a kinder word than *work*.) First to Him, and then to others. Remember, to serve others is to serve God. To serve God is an act of worship and a confirmation of our devotion to Him. The more we do it, the more enjoyable it becomes as we begin to experience the blessings that come our way when we choose to serve for no other reason than because we are in love.

MICHELLE MCKINNEY HAMMOND
A SASSY GIRL'S GUIDE TO LOVING GOD

There Is No "I" in Team

You can easily enough see how this kind of thing
works by looking no further than your own body.
Your body has many parts—limbs, organs, cells—
but no matter how many parts you can name,
you're still one body. It's exactly the same with Christ.

1 Corinthians 12:12 MSG

Is your nickname "Tammy Takeover"? Do you try to do everything alone? If so, we should form a support group—because I also struggle with that I'll-just-do-it myself attitude.

Of course, that line of thinking isn't original. The world has been telling us for years, "If you want something done right, you have to do it yourself." So I decided I would. I tried to do it all—all by myself—all the time. I ended up overwrought, stressed, and mean.

God didn't intend for us to go it alone. He even addresses that errant line of thinking in 1 Corinthians 12:12, using the human body as an example of teamwork.

We are just one part of the big picture. We each play an important role, but we will never accomplish what God has for us if we try to do everything all alone. No matter what a great eyeball you are, you will never be able to hear, because you're not an ear!

So quit trying to be an ear! Be the best eyeball you can be, and work with the person in your life who was called to be an ear. Together, you will do much! Alone, you will just be a good eye—nothing more. Lose the "Tammy Takeover" mentality and do your part with the rest of the body, and big things can be accomplished in a short time. And the really great part is that you will be much happier! You will get to enjoy the experience and celebrate with the team members when meet goals are met. It's a win/win situation.

MICHELLE MEDLOCK ADAMS
SECRETS OF HAPPINESS

The Confidence to Serve

In Joppa there was a follower named Tabitha.
Her Greek name was Dorcas, which means "deer."
She was always doing good things for people
and had given much to the poor.

ACTS 9:36 CEV

From the time that Jesus began His ministry through the travels of His disciples, Scripture is filled with people who came to them, asking for healing. Dorcas, on the other hand, never seemed to ask for anything. Instead, her heart was set on serving.

Dorcas lived in Joppa, a seacoast town about thirty-five miles from Jerusalem. Losing a husband or son was a frequent occurrence for the women there. Although she was a widow herself, Dorcas kept moving forward with her life, "doing good things," and providing widows in need with clothes she had sewn herself.

No wonder, then, that when she suddenly died, the believers in Joppa who adored her immediately sent for Peter. When he arrived, the widows grabbed him, showing Peter the garments she'd made for them. Peter was moved by their devotion, and he sent them away. Kneeling by her bed to pray, Peter called her name and said simply, "Arise."

She did, and Peter presented her to the other widows. Before long, everyone in the area knew about her healing, which resulted in many of them coming to the Lord.

Being a servant is not easy. But when that work is done in the name of the Lord, even the simplest skill can become a great tool for evangelism. Servanthood is a gift, and Dorcas clearly demonstrated that when we have the confidence to serve in small ways, great things can be the result.

RAMONA RICHARDS
SECRETS OF CONFIDENCE

The Freedom of Forgiveness

If you forgive men their trespasses,
your heavenly Father will also forgive you.

MATTHEW 6:14 NKJV

Everything we do in life that has eternal value hinges on two things: loving God and loving others. It's far easier to love God than it is to love others, but God sees them as being the same. One of the most loving things we can do is forgive. It's hard to forgive those who have hurt, offended, or mistreated us. But God wants us to love even our enemies. And in the process of doing so, He perfects us.

It's always going to be easy to find things to be unforgiving about. We have to stop looking. Forgiveness opens your heart and mind and allows the Holy Spirit to work freely in you. It releases you to love God more and feel His love in greater measure. Life is worth nothing without that.

STORMIE OMARTIAN
THE POWER OF PRAYING

Lonely No More

God places the lonely in families.

PSALM 68:6 NLT

Kate moved to a new, unfamiliar town and soon found herself spending her Friday evenings alone with her cat, television, and a carton of double chocolate fudge ice cream. After one particularly lonely Friday, she planned ahead and found a local soup kitchen that needed volunteers. Instead of drowning her sorrows in ice cream, Kate found a whole new community of amazing people to love.

We've all endured a few depressing Friday nights, but that's not what God desires for us. In Genesis 2:18 (MSG) God said, "It's not good for the Man to be alone; I'll make him a helper, a companion." We were created to live in community. We often apply this verse to marriage, but singles weren't meant to be alone either.

Before the next lonely Friday night sneaks up on you, consider some creative acts of service that can bring new community into your life. Is there a homeless shelter that needs your help? Perhaps you know a shut-in who would like some company. Nursing homes and retirement communities are always looking for volunteers to brighten the lives of their residents.

Being lonely is no fun. But the world is also full of lonely people—people who can experience the love of the Father by spending an evening with you.

JOANNA BLOSS
DAILY ENCOURAGEMENT FOR SINGLE WOMEN

Moments of Heavenly Humor

A merry heart does good, like medicine,
but a broken spirit dries the bones.

PROVERBS 17:22 NKJV

One of my friends is especially good at helping me find the heavenly humor when things go wrong. For example, last year when I lost my credit card, I was dreading the ordeal of reporting it and getting it replaced, but she told me, "Oh, Barb, don't be upset. Maybe you'll find your card. And if you don't, I'll bet something happens while you're looking for it that will make you laugh and then you'll have another funny story to share with someone else who needs a little splash of joy."

I rolled my eyes and started looking for the credit card company's phone number. . . . Finally I called the bank that had issued the card. Six menu options later, I was once again speaking to a real person. . . .

"Just call the number on the back of the card," she told me hurriedly.

"Excuse me?" I asked.

"If you'll turn the card over, you'll see a line that says, 'For lost or stolen cards, call this number.'" And with that, she hung up!

"How can I turn the card over and call the number on the back if I've *lost* the card?" I barked at the world in general. . . . Then I laughed, and there it was: the moment my friend had predicted.

How blessed I am to have such a precious friend who knows just how to offer hope no matter what stressful situation I find myself in.

BARBARA JOHNSON
LAUGHTER FROM HEAVEN

Paul's Prayer for the Jews

*Brethren, my heart's desire and my prayer
to God for them is for their salvation.*

Romans 10:1 NASB

Is the deepest concern of your heart that those whom you love will share heaven with Christ? The deepest longing of Paul's soul was that the Jews might know their Messiah. Paul longed for the Israelites, "to whom belongs the adoption as sons, and the glory and the covenants and the giving of the Law and the temple service and the promises," to understand that Christ had come to save them (Romans 9:4 NASB).

The Jews couldn't truly be God's children until they partook of the light of truth. "For the Scripture says, 'Whoever believes in Him will not be disappointed.' For there is no distinction between Jew and Greek; for the same Lord is Lord of all, abounding in riches for all who call on Him; for 'Whoever will call on the name of the Lord will be saved'" (Romans 10:11–13 NASB).

Paul presents the simple process by which they can become cleansed of their sins. "But what does it say? 'The word is near you, in your mouth and in your heart'—that is, the word of faith which we are preaching, that if you confess with your mouth Jesus as Lord, and believe in your heart that God raised Him from the dead, you will be saved; for with the heart a person believes, resulting in righteousness, and with the mouth he confesses, resulting in salvation" (Romans 10:8–10 NASB).

CAROL L. FITZPATRICK
DAILY WISDOM FOR WOMEN

Catching Up with God

I wish for the days when I was strong,
when God's close friendship blessed my house.

JOB 29:4 NCV

You know how friends can become emotionally separated when they don't see each other and communicate frequently? Well, it's the same with you and God. If you don't keep in touch with Him, you begin to feel distant from Him even when you're not. This is why you must pray daily. Also, when you spend time with someone you respect, the character of that person rubs off on you. When you are in the presence of God, His character is formed *in* you. . . .

We can't receive God's best for our lives, and we can't push back the things that were never God's will for us, except through prayer. We have to remember the many reasons to pray. . .and get in the habit of not making prayer a last resort. We have to learn that we can't leave our life to chance. We have to pray about everything all the time, not just when things go wrong. We have to pray over anything that concerns us, no matter how big—"With God nothing will be impossible" (Luke 1:37 NKJV)—or how small—"The very hairs of your head are all numbered" (Matthew 10:30 NKJV).

STORMIE OMARTIAN
FINDING PEACE FOR YOUR HEART

Gossip Doesn't Pay

A gossip separates close friends.

PROVERBS 16:28 NIV

If you've ever had someone gossip about you, you know why this verse is in the Bible. Put a bunch of people together in the same office or on the same job site, and sooner or later the whispering starts. "Did you hear about. . . ?" or "I heard that Mary. . ." People just can't seem to resist talking about one another.

What may start out as "innocent information" can quickly damage reputations and cause hurt among friends. It can destroy even a close friendship. God warns against gossip because it breaks relationships. He doesn't care if it's "true gossip" or a pack of lies—spreading news of other people is not part of the biblical code.

So when you hear something that you "just have to tell"

someone, put one hand over your mouth, bite your tongue, or do whatever you must to keep your mouth shut. Ask God to give you self-control, because you don't want to break up a friendship—especially your friendship with Him.

PAMELA L. McQUADE
DAILY WISDOM FOR THE WORKPLACE

Friendships Take Time

*A friend is always loyal, and a brother
is born to help in time of need.*

PROVERBS 17:17 NLT

Patty frowned as she hung up the phone. She knew that
a one-hour get-together really meant three hours. She
didn't have that kind of time in her day! Her to-do list was
already two pages long. But Patty could tell by the tone of
her friend's voice that she was troubled and needed to talk.

Oh, why can't friendships be more efficient? Patty
wondered to herself, not for the first time. She loved her
friends, but her spare time was in short supply. It was so
valuable!

But relationships are valuable, too. And they take
time to be nourished so they will develop into a satisfying
experience. Isn't the entire Bible an analogy of God's

patience, wooing us into a deeper relationship with Himself? God knew that nothing can satisfy us like a relationship with Him. To woo us, He gives us His time and attention, the kind of focus that can touch our hearts.

True intimacy cannot be rushed or scheduled or abbreviated or economized. It just takes time.

Suzanne Woods Fisher
Whispers of Wisdom for Busy Women

Strength in Numbers

Be anxious for nothing, but in everything by prayer
and supplication, with thanksgiving,
let your requests be made known to God.

PHILIPPIANS 4:6 NKJV

I know of a small group of boys and girls in America who met together in the mornings to pray. They had seen lots of things go wrong at school. They soon noticed that the atmosphere in their class improved greatly after they had prayed. More and more young Christians joined them. After a time, they were forbidden to use the room. They looked for a quiet place where they could pray and found a cemetery near the school.

Winter came. They were very cold at the cemetery, but they carried on. One day the principal saw the students coming from the cemetery, and he asked them what they were doing there. They said that the cemetery was the only quiet place they could find where they could pray undisturbed. The principal was so touched that he opened a pleasant room for them where they could hold their prayer meeting each day. And that continues regularly. Miracles happen in that school. Instead of constant arguments between teachers and pupils, there is an atmosphere of unity. The principal told me this and said that he was sure this was the answer to the boys' and girls' prayers.

CORRIE TEN BOOM
REFLECTIONS OF GOD'S GLORY

Birth of a Friendship

For the LORD is good; His mercy is everlasting,
and His truth endures to all generations.

PSALM 100:5 NKJV

Dismay blanketed the office as news spread from cubicle to cubicle: the wife of one of our favorite co-workers had just lost her baby.

I slipped into the bathroom and wiped empathetic tears for his wife, Suzanne. I had miscarried the year before and understood the grief of preempted parenting.

Though I'd never met Suzanne, I wrote this young Christian mother a letter which said all the things I wished someone had said to me.

Suzanne wrote back. Our friendship was instant and deep, a sisterly bond forged by common hurt and common belief in the One who shared our troubles. Over the following year, we spent lots of time together, a couple of modern-day Hannahs trying to catch God's attention, and eventually the giggles outweighed the tears.

As we were about to discover, our Father was listening to every word.

"I'm going to have a baby!" Suzanne's bubbly voice danced over the phone line. I celebrated like I was the one who was pregnant.

A week later, I was.

A dozen years have passed since that glorious day when God filled both our arms with cherub-cheeked treasure. Suzanne and I now smile at our precocious preteens and their equally adored older siblings, keenly aware of how special each one of them is. . .just like our other children, who are playing at Jesus' house until their mommies come home.

CHERYL GOCHNAUER
KISSES OF SUNSHINE FOR WOMEN

Honey to the Soul

Kind words are like honey—
sweet to the soul and healthy for the body.

PROVERBS 16:24 NLT

One of the great blessings of the Christian life is a kind word, spoken just when you need to hear it.

Look at the unbelieving world, and how often will you find kindness? Once in awhile, in a rare human being. More often, you'll experience criticism and condemnation.

One thing that should set Christians apart from unbelievers is a caring kindness. When you don't find kindness in the church, something has gone wrong. A critical spirit isn't from God and can't help the soul and body.

But we also can't expect the church always to agree with all we do. When we've fallen into wrongdoing, it is the responsibility of caring Christians to confront us lovingly and set us on the right track. When we respond to that correction, we can again feel the kindness of those who have loved us well enough to tell us we've been wrong. We might have missed it when we were doing wrong, but wise Christians will still have used it to draw us back to the right path.

People have a hard time hearing critics, unless they know care is also there. A combination of correction and kindness often makes the difference in whether or not those words are really heard. Honey spreads easily on the soul, while criticism feels like sand in an open wound.

Whether you need to encourage or redirect another Christian, are you speaking kind words? If so, their sweetness may bring just the healing God has in mind.

PAMELA MCQUADE
DAILY WISDOM TO SATISFY THE SOUL

Be Yourself

*"Do you want to stand out? Then step down.
Be a servant. If you puff yourself up, you'll get the wind
knocked out of you. But if you're content to simply
be yourself, your life will count for plenty."*

MATTHEW 23:11 MSG

$\mathcal{M}$aybe you too have exhausted yourself striving to be sweeter or thinner or a better scrapbooker. Perhaps you've crafted Bible study answers with the goal of impressing the girls in your small group. It's easy to fall prey to the feel-good addiction of other people's approval.

Sadly, after twenty years in vocational ministry, I've realized that many of us are just as prone to perform for God as for anyone else. You've probably noticed people putting on their best behavior at church—or perhaps caught yourself doing the same thing. Like kids playing dress-up, we pretend to be glossier versions of ourselves, as if we're afraid we won't make it into "God's club" unless we put on a good show.

On those days—or weeks!—when we feel like we don't measure up, like our lives are one long blooper reel, we can find hope in what King David wrote in Psalm 139: "You have searched me, LORD, and you know me" (Psalm 139:1 NIV).

LISA HARPER
A PERFECT MESS

Glimpsing the Image of Christ

To them God has chosen to make known among the Gentiles the glorious riches of this mystery, which is Christ in you, the hope of glory.

COLOSSIANS 1:27 NIV

We shall not be fully changed into the image of Christ until He shall appear, and we shall "see him as he is." But meanwhile, according to our measure, the life of Jesus is to be made "manifest in our mortal flesh." Is it made manifest in ours? Are we so "conformed to the image" of Christ that men in seeing us see a glimpse of Him also?

A Methodist minister's wife told me that at one time, when they had moved to a new place, her little boy came in after the first afternoon of play, and exclaimed joyfully, "Oh, Mother, I have found such a lovely, good little girl to play with, that I never want to go away again."

"I am very glad, darling," said the loving mother, happy over her child's happiness. "What is the little girl's name?"

"Oh," replied the child, with a sudden solemnity, "I think her name is Jesus."

"Why, Frank!" exclaimed the horrified mother. "What do you mean?"

"Well, Mother," he said deprecatingly, "she was so lovely that I did not know what she could be called but Jesus."

Are our lives so Christlike that anyone could have such a thought of us? Is it patent to all around us that we have been with Jesus? Is it not, alas, often just the contrary? Are not some of us so cross and uncomfortable in our living that exactly the opposite thing would have to be said about us?

HANNAH WHITALL SMITH
THE GOD OF ALL COMFORT

Kindness: A Way of Life

Put on therefore, as the elect of God, holy and beloved,
bowels of mercies, kindness, humbleness of mind, meekness,
longsuffering. . . . And above all these things put on charity,
which is the bond of perfectness.

COLOSSIANS 3:12, 14 KJV

The President and I had not gone many yards before I heard the familiar voice of an old domestic to whom I was indebted for many favors. The dear old woman was not at that time in the employ of the Institution, but had just returned for a few minutes to speak with some of us; and I knew that I might not see her again for months to come. This thought was uppermost in my mind at that moment; and so I turned impulsively to President Polk and said, "Will you please excuse me a minute?"

Realizing my discourtesy on my return, I made all manner of apologies. To my surprise, however, the great and good man said, "You have done well, and I commend you for it. Kindness, even to those in the humblest capacity of life, should be our rule of conduct; and by this act you have won not only my respect but also my esteem." I had hitherto held a high opinion of President Polk but from that moment his kind words elevated him to my own ideal of a Christian gentleman.

FANNY CROSBY
MEMORIES OF EIGHTY YEARS

Above All Else, Love

Be completely humble and gentle; be patient,
bearing with one another in love. Make every effort
to keep the unity of the Spirit through the bond of peace.

EPHESIANS 4:2–3 NIV

Although love is the greatest commandment we have,
sometimes it can be the hardest. There are many people
who can be difficult to love. Paul must have dealt with this:
He tells us to be patient and bear one another in love.

I have come across many people whom I found hard
to love. Some at school, some at work, and, believe it or
not, some at church. It is so easy to see the faults in others
though it is usually very difficult to see the faults in our
own lives. The same people I may have had a hard time
loving may have had an even harder time loving me!

God has created us all different; how boring it would

be if we were all the same. However, our difference is sometimes followed with complications. Remember we have no idea what could be going on in that person's life to make them so hard to love. If we can learn to humble ourselves and be patient and gentle, God will help us see the common bond we have in the Spirit. He will empower us to love them. God is love, and He has called us to make every effort to keep the unity of the Spirit.

SARAH HOSTETLER
CIRCLE OF FRIENDS

Freedom to Love

So this is my prayer: that your love will flourish and that you will not only love much but well. Learn to love appropriately.

PHILIPPIANS 1:9 MSG

The more you receive the love of God, the more it flows through you to others. In fact, our love of other people is the most compelling sign of all to an unbeliever. It was the love of God I saw in other people that drew me toward the Lord. It is the love of God in me that has filled me with love for others—even people in other places whom I don't know. Jesus said, "A new commandment I give to you, that you love one another; as I have loved you, that you also love one another" (John 13:34 NKJV). Jesus loved us so much that He laid down His life for us. We don't have to die for others, but we can lay down our life in other ways.

The Bible says that if we don't have love in our heart for others, we have nothing and whatever good we think we do, we will not benefit from it. "Though I speak with the tongues of men and of angels, but have not love, I have become sounding brass or a clanging cymbal. . . . And though I have all faith, so that I could remove mountains, but have not love, I am nothing" (1 Corinthians 13:1–2 NKJV). God wants to fill your heart with His love so that you can extend it to others.

STORMIE OMARTIAN
THE POWER OF A PRAYING LIFE

Title Index

Contributors

Michelle Medlock Adams has a diverse résumé featuring inspirational books, children's picture books, and greeting cards. Her insights have appeared in periodicals across America, including *Today's Christian Woman* and *Guideposts for Kids*. She lives in Fort Worth, Texas, with her husband, two daughters, and a "mini petting zoo."

Beth Beechy is married to her high school sweetheart, Brian, and they have five delightful children. A mostly stay-at-home mom, Beth works part-time as a bookkeeper. A founding board member of Circle of Friends, she gives her time to COF's radio program, worship team, prayer ministry, and GirlFriends events.

Emily Biggers is a gifted education specialist in a north Texas public school district. She enjoys traveling, freelance writing, and serving in a local apartment ministry through her church.

Joanna Bloss is a personal trainer, writer, and student living in the Midwest. She is a coauthor of *Grit for the Oyster: 250 Pearls of Wisdom for Aspiring Authors*.

Corrie ten Boom (1892–1983) was simply an ordinary, middle-aged Dutch spinster when the Second World War began. By the time the conflict ended, she was literally transformed by the faith she had merely accepted and on a mission from God. By God's grace, Corrie survived the concentration camp and became a "tramp for the Lord," sharing in more than sixty nations the thrilling message that nothing, not even death, can separate us from God's love.

Patsy Clairmont is a speaker with Women of Faith conferences and bestselling author of a number of books including *God Uses Cracked Pots* and *Normal Is Just a Setting on the Dryer*. In her speaking career she has blessed over four million women with her humor, vitality, and scriptural knowledge.

Fanny Crosby (1820–1915), blinded at infancy, became one of the most popular and prolific of all hymn writers. She wrote more than eight thousand hymns in her lifetime, including the best-known "Blessed Assurance," "Jesus Is Tenderly Calling You Home," "Praise Him, Praise Him," and "To God Be the Glory."

Hayley DiMarco has written cutting-edge books like *Mean Girls: Facing Your Beauty*, the bestselling *Dateable: Are You? Are They?* and *The Dirt on Breaking Up*, among others. Her goal is to give practical answers for life's problems and encourage people into stronger spiritual lives. Hayley founded Hungry Planet, a think tank that feeds the world's appetite for truth through authors, speakers, and consultants. For more info on Hungry Planet, check out www.hungryplanet.net.

Elisabeth Elliot is a bestselling author of more than twenty books including *Passion and Purity*, *Be Still My Soul*, *The Path of Loneliness*, and *Keep a Quiet Heart*. She and her husband, Lars Gren, make their home in Magnolia, Massachusetts.

Suzanne Woods Fisher is an author and contributing editor to *Christian Parenting Today* magazine. Her debut novel, *Copper Star*, was released in 2007. The sequel, *Copper Fire*, was released in May 2008.

Carol L. Fitzpatrick is a bestselling author of nine books that have totaled nearly three-quarters of a million books sold. She is a frequent conference speaker for writing groups and church groups. Carol and her husband have three grown children and three grandchildren. Although she credits her Midwest upbringing for instilling her core values, she has lived in California for nearly four decades.

Cheryl Gochnauer is the founder of Homebodies (www.homebodies.org), an online and print ministry for present and prospective stay-at-home moms, and the author of *Stay-at-Home Handbook: Advice on Parenting, Finances, Career, Surviving Each Day & Much More.*

Mary Graham is president of Women of Faith (WOF), a division of Thomas Nelson, Inc., which hosts America's largest women's conference. Since 1996, over three million women have attended Women of Faith conferences in eighty cities. A graduate of California State University in sociology, she has lived in many parts of the United States and her work has taken her to every continent.

Mabel Hale lived in Wichita, Kansas, in the early twentieth century. *Beautiful Girlhood* was her most popular book.

Michelle McKinney Hammond is a bestselling author, speaker, singer, and television cohost. She has authored more than thirty books including the bestselling titles *The Diva Principle*; *Sassy, Single, and Satisfied*; *101 Ways to Get and Keep His Attention*; and *Secrets of an Irresistible Woman*. She makes her home in Chicago.

Janice Hanna, who lives in the Houston area, writes novels, nonfiction, magazine articles, and musical comedies for the stage. The mother of four married daughters, she is quickly adding grandchildren to the family mix.

Lisa Harper is a communicator, author, speaker, and Bible teacher. She has spoken at Women of Faith, Moody Bible, Winsome Women, and Focus on the Family conferences and has written a number of books including *A Perfect Mess: How God Adores and Transforms Imperfect People Like Us*.

Frances Ridley Havergal (1836–1879) was an English poet and hymn writer. "Take My Life and Let It Be" is one of her best-known hymns. She also wrote hymn melodies, religious tracts, and works for children.

Missy Horsfall is a published magazine and greeting card writer and coauthor of the novel *Love Me Back to Life*. A pastor's wife, she is a speaker and Bible study teacher for Circle of Friends and serves on the board overseeing its writing ministries. Missy also produces and cohosts the COF radio program.

Sarah Hostetler grew up in Ohio and now resides with her husband, Travis, in Huntersville, North Carolina. She enjoys writing and studying God's Word. Sarah writes devotionals for the Circle of Friends website, www.circleoffriends.fm.

Sharon Jaynes is the author of thirteen books with Harvest House Publishers, Focus on the Family, and Moody Publishers and a frequent guest on national radio and television. She has also written numerous magazine articles and devotions for publications such as *Focus on the Family*, *Decision*, *Crosswalk.com*, and *In Touch*.

Barbara Johnson (1927–2007) was an award-winning author and Women of Faith Speaker emeritus with more than four million books in print and translated into ten foreign languages. She faced her long battle with cancer with the same humor and wisdom with which she met the many adversities of her life.

Jackie M. Johnson is a freelance writer and marketing copywriter for companies and faith-based organizations such as Compassion International, Focus on the Family, and Young Life. She lives in Colorado Springs, Colorado.

Austine Keller resides in Tampa, Florida, writing and publishing as a ministry to others as well as for her own enjoyment. She also enjoys a newly emptied nest and fishing with her husband.

Carol Kent is an internationally known speaker and author. Her books include *When I Lay My Isaac Down*, *Becoming a Woman of Influence*, and *Mothers Have Angel Wings*. She is president of Speak Up Speaker Services and the founder and director of Speak Up with Confidence seminars.

Virelle Kidder is a full-time writer and conference speaker and author of six books including *Meet Me at the Well* and *The Best Life Ain't Easy*. She is published in national magazines such as *Moody Magazine*, Focus on the Family's *Pastor's Family*, *Decision*, *Pray!*, *Journey*, *HomeLife*, and *Tapestry*.

Tina Krause is an award-winning newspaper columnist and author of the book *Laughter Therapy*. She is a wife, mom, and grandmother of four. Tina and her husband, Jim, live in Valparaiso, Indiana.

Donna K. Maltese is a freelance writer, editor, and proofreader; publicist for a local Mennonite project; and the assistant director of RevWriter Writers Conferences. Donna resides in Bucks County, Pennsylvania, with her husband and two children. She is a pastor's prayer partner and is active in her local church.

Pamela L. McQuade is a freelance writer and editor in Nutley, New Jersey, who has worked with numerous publishers. Her Barbour credits include *The Word on Life*,

Daily Wisdom for Couples, and *Prayers and Promises*, all coauthored with Toni Sortor. Pam and her husband share their home with basset hounds and are involved in basset hound rescue.

Shari Minke is an inspirational author, speaker, humorist, and dramatist using biblical teaching, humorous characters, and Bible dramas to impart scriptural principles. She and her husband, Tom, live in Novi, Michigan, have four grown children, and are thrilled to be called grandparents.

Stormie Omartian is a popular writer, speaker, and author. She is author of the bestselling *The Power of Praying*® books as well as many other titles. She and her husband have been married thirty years and have three grown children.

Donna Partow is an author and motivational speaker. Her books, including *This Isn't the Life I Signed Up For. . .But I'm Finding Hope and Healing* and *Becoming a Vessel God Can Use*, have sold almost a million copies, and her ministry Pieces4Peace reaches into the largest Muslim city in the world.

Rachel Quillin lives with her husband, Eric, and their six

children on a dairy farm in Ohio. Her main focus is to serve the Lord in any way possible. She is active in her church, enjoys homeschooling her kids, doing freelance writing, and is never bored!

Ramona Richards is a freelance writer and editor living in Tennessee. Formerly the editor of *Ideals* magazine, Ramona has also edited children's books, fiction, nonfiction, study Bibles, and reference books for major Christian publishers. She is the author of *A Moment with God for Single Parents*.

Bobbie Rill is a motivational speaker and life coach. As a Licensed Professional Counselor, she served as executive director over a multistate network of Christian counseling and educational centers. She also directed Women of Virtue, a national conference and radio ministry. She and her husband, Bob, reside in Tucson, Arizona.

Frances J. Roberts (1918–2009) is best known for her classic devotional *Come Away My Beloved*. She founded The King's Press in 1964, where she authored and published *Come Away* and eight other books, selling over 1.5 million copies in the last thirty years.

Allison L. Shaw is a freelance writer and editor from Sacramento, California. She is passionate about children's literature, her career as a librarian, and her husband, Michael. Her published work appears in the *Sacramento Bee*, several anthologies, and pages scattered throughout the World Wide Web.

Hannah Whitall Smith (1832–1911) was born into a strict Quaker home in Philadelphia and became a major influence in the Holiness movement of the late nineteenth century. Besides *The Christian's Secret of a Happy Life*, Smith also wrote *The God of All Comfort* and an autobiography, *The Unselfishness of God and How I Discovered It*.

Luci Swindoll, one of Women of Faith's original speakers, has been inspiring women across North America for twelve years now. Author, speaker, photographer, musician, and artist, Luci currently resides in Texas.

Sheila Walsh is a unique combination of international author, speaker, worship leader, television talk show host, and Bible teacher. She is a speaker with Women of Faith and bestselling author of her memoir, *Honestly*, and the Gold Medallion Award nominee *The Heartache No One Sees*.

Permissions

Scripture Index

OLD TESTAMENT

NEW TESTAMENT

What Is Circle of Friends?

Circle of Friends Ministries, Inc., is a nonprofit organization established to build a pathway for women to come into a personal relationship with Jesus Christ and to build Christian unity among women. Our mission is to honor Jesus Christ through meeting the needs of women in our local, national, and international communities. Our vision is to be women who are committed to Jesus Christ, obediently seeking God's will and fulfilling our life mission as Christ followers. As individuals and as a corporate group, we minister a Christ-centered hope, biblically based encouragement, and unconditional love by offering God-honoring, Word-based teaching, worship, accountability, and fellowship to women in a nondenominational environment through speaker services, worship teams, daily Weblogs and devotionals, radio programs, and GirlFriends teen events.

COF also partners with churches and women's groups to bring conferences, retreats, Bible studies, concerts, simulcasts, and servant evangelism projects to their communities. We have a Marketplace Ministry teaching kingdom principles in the workplace and are committed to undergird, with prayer and financial support, foreign mission projects that impact the world for Jesus Christ. Our goal is to evangelize the lost and edify the body of Christ by touching the lives of women—locally, nationally, and globally.

What Is Circle of Friends?

Circle of Friends Ministries, Inc., is a nonprofit organization established to build a pathway for women to come into a personal relationship with Jesus Christ and to build Christian unity among women. Our mission is to honor Jesus Christ through meeting the needs of women in our local, national, and international communities. Our vision is to be women who are committed to Jesus Christ, obediently seeking God's will and fulfilling our life mission as Christ followers. As individuals and as a corporate group, we minister a Christ-centered hope, biblically based encouragement, and unconditional love by offering God-honoring, Word-based teaching, worship, accountability, and fellowship to women in a nondenominational environment through speaker services, worship teams, daily Weblogs and devotionals, radio programs, and GirlFriends teen events.

COF also partners with churches and women's groups to bring conferences, retreats, Bible studies, concerts, simulcasts, and servant evangelism projects to their communities. We have a Marketplace Ministry teaching kingdom principles in the workplace and are committed to undergird, with prayer and financial support, foreign mission projects that impact the world for Jesus Christ. Our goal is to evangelize the lost and edify the body of Christ by touching the lives of women—locally, nationally, and globally.